Grooming the Middle

Life and Perspective in the Novels of E.M. Forster

Grooming the Middle

Life and Perspective in the Novels of E.M. Forster

A.A. Khan
S. Mansoor Ali

ADHYAYAN

ADHYAYAN PUBLISHERS & DISTRIBUTORS
New Delhi-110002

Published by
ADHYAYAN PUBLISHERS & DISTRIBUTORS
4378/4B, 105, J.M.D. House, Murari Lal Street
Ansari Road Darya Ganj, New Delhi - 110002
Ph.: 011-23263018, 011-23277156, Fax: 23280028
Email: adhyayanpublishers@yahoo.com

Grooming the Middle:
Life and Perspective in the
Novels of E.M. Forster

Edition 2011
ISBN 978-81-8435-305-1

Printed in India

Published by Harish Chandra Yadav for Adhyayan Publishers & Distributors, Delhi. Laser Typesetting at Jain Computers and Printed at Tarun Offset Printers, Delhi

This Book is
Dedicated to my
beloved Parents

Late Mohammad Ali

(Advocate)

and

Late Sarwari Md. Ali

- Dr. S. Mansoor Ali

Acknowledgements

We are obliged to our relatives, teachers, friends, colleagues, whose continuous encouragement and prayers kept us committed to our work. We genuinely thank them all.

We are greatly indebted to acknowledge the co-operation received from Dr. (Mrs.) Qamar Talat, Professor, Department of English, Govt. V.Y.T.P.G. Autonomous College, Durg (C.G.) for her constant support and encouragement.

We place our thanks to Adhyayan Publishers and Distributors, New Delhi for readily accepting to publish this book in such a nice form.

Durg
Date-17-02-2011

Dr. A.A. Khan
Dr. S. Mansoor Ali

Preface

E.M. Forster's philosophy of life is the subject of the present study. His five published novels cover a wide range, extending from social comedy to fantasy and fantasy to prophesy. G.M. Trevelyan has rightly described Forster's fiction as an "art in which he is perhaps our greatest living master:' His ideas and believes particularly in "A Passage to India" have starting affinity with Indian thought which has always been strongly dominated by concern with the inner life and self of man. Forster the creative artist, is deeply concerned with the inner life of the individual and the 'subjective' becomes the focus of interest in his fiction.

As a writer of fiction, Forster is concerned with three important aspect of novel—Life, Philosophy and Form. In his first four novels, he is baffled by his inner tensions and moral dilemmas struggling against the stresses and the strains of bourgeois life in Edwardian England, he tries to seek harmony which he finally achieve in "A Passage to India". His philosophy seems to cover the entire range of human experience from paganism to modern scepticism. Forster's value of life which form the core of his philosophy are compassion, the life of the spirit and a belief in the worth of the individual. Forster respond quickly and warmly to human suffering. He believes that the self of man is true and invincible and he pleads vigorously for the autonomy of individual.

His novels deals with the basic themes of personal

relationships, conflict between the inner and the outer life, search for identity and especially his social ideas are far reaching and generous.

Forster's view on India, his lifelong suspicion of the metaphysical and his sceptical humanism so plainly present in 'Abinger Harvest,' besides the mystical and oriental element in his mental make up have been taken into consideration in the present study. The personal records and the documents of the contemporaries writers, the journal of Amid Bennett and H.S. Wells' Experiment in Autobiography and books on the English novel – F.R. Leavis the Great tradition Edwin Muris's The Structure of the Novel and Arnold Kettel's, "An Introduction to the English Novel" have been examined and discussed with a view to throwing light of Forster's method and technique.

Although critics have studied the novel of Forester from diverse view point yet there is a good deal of scope for the assessment of his philosophy from a new angle. The present study is an attempt to focus attention on the basic features of his philosophy, such as, the aspect of Forster's various themes his treatment of English middle-class, his humanism and his point of view.

The first chapter deals with the various themes of his novels. The value of a work of art depends upon prime sensibility clearness of perception and sensitiveness. Forster has made the theme of personal relationships, struggle for total spirituality are significant in an age of cross materialism. The theme of personal relationship based on private affection, tender heartedness and secret understanding of the heart. The philosophy of Forster is directed to the basic theme of his novels. It is the true self that gives meaning of life, it is the tender core of the heart that creates personal relationships. Forster's philosophy revealed in his bringing out the contrast between two modes of life – the conventional and the natural in Where Angle.... His anti-medieval outlook is seen in A Room ... where he glorifies love and condemn the medieval concept of asceticism and celibacy. The Longest Journey deals with the theme of reality and quest for originality. His individualistic approach to life is evident in Howard End where he wants to connect the outer life with the inner. And finally his prophetic vision is evident in A Passage.... The social theme takes the form of Satire and the comedy of manners, the nature theme, the form of fantasy: while the theme of appearance and reality takes the form of prophesy.

In the third chapter an attempt has been made to examine the social vision and his treatment of English middle class.. The novel deals with the life of man society, and it also deals with the life of man centred in the spiritual reality. The vision of Forster is social as well as imaginative. Social comedy works within the framework of conventions. The social vision of the novelist exposes vanity, selfishness, greed, hypocrisy, diplomacy and insincerity which form the armour of falsehood. The eternal theme of social comedy is the clash between illusion and reality. Behind the satire of Forster there lies a vision of the good life. So, this chapter will point out the Forster's criticism to English hypocrisy and he also defines the problem of the English middle-class.

In the fourth chapter, E.M. Forster is regarded as a liberal humanist. This chapter will point out the definition and interpretation of the word "Liberal & Humanist. Forster is regarded as 'liberal' because he compromises between the changing values of life and the old tradition of contemporary England. It was the liberalism of mid-Victorian period, which supported freedom of enterprise and free trade, advocated local self-government, practiced benevolence, uphold free speech, introduced social reforms, and entertained a sincere faith in the progress of society. The humanist considers this world as real, emphasized the dignity of man and the worth of human life, tends to place reason, above revelation, and stress on self-education and self-development. Humanism, in fact makes for tolerance, equilibrium and sanity. The novelist as a humanist, shows curiosity of a free mind, belief in good taste and belief in human race. Forster as a individualist always lays stress on the humanistic values, that really do matter, tolerance, good temper and sympathy, the natural warmth of relations, the worth of individual and love for all types of man. This chapter will throw light on his basic humanistic ideas and thought as reflected in his major novels.

In the fifth chapter E.M. Forsters' A Passage to India' is a major document as a study of imperialist propaganda, polemic against British rule in India. 'A Passage to India' provides a complex study of relationship between individual and communal, between the English and the Indians. Englishmen are not only different on the point of view of physical appearance but they are different on the point of view of there psychology thought and feelings as they reflected towards the Indians. They regarded Indians as something dull and inhuman. In this dealings with Indian, the British, as a class, operate only at the level of political and social duty. Forster sees the British rule as a corrupting influence on both the ruler and the ruled. One more important question which Forster arise in this novel is whether it is possible for an Indian to be a friend with an English man. And Dr. Aziz says on the behalf of the Indians that without equality, no, never.

So, this chapter will point out the differences between values of East (Indian) and the West (British).

The sixth chapter deals with the Forster's technique and his ideas about plot and characters. The novelist find disorder in life but he imposes order on it by an act of imagination. Technique is needed, but not at the expense of content and imaginative vision. It is needed for selecting and processing the raw material into a coherent form. A new technique is based on the novelist's original creative impulse. Technique alters from generation to generation and each artist has to discover the device or the method which particularly suits him and his subject-matter. The novelist succeeds in his mission if, by the technique of non-didactic fiction, he moves his reader into a new order of perception. Technique — whether it is defined as "process" or "discovery" or "rhetoric" is necessary and its value as a shaping instrument has to be acknowledged. All the methods are good provided they are effective.

In the last chapter, Forster's philosophy of life as reflected in his novels is summarized. Forster is a traditionalist who regards the story, the plot, the characters and the social scene as the essential aspects of the novel. Truth, the moral philosophy of his novels, enhances the significance of life. His novels are characterized by a freshness of outlook. The warmth of human love, the passion for truth, the awareness of self, the glow of the inner life, the loyalty to the inner convictions and the allegiance to the free spirit are the values that really matter in life. His philosophy regarded as humanistic. Because he thinks for mankind firstly. Man is the supreme creation of nature and everything is relates to its. Forster knows it very well. His major themes of his novels all directed by his philosophy of life, which is the main power of Forster. His philosophy contain all those human values which mankind has cherished from time immemorial.

Contents

1

Introduction

(A) The Age of E.M. Forster

Normally the Victorean era closes in 1900, actually it came to an end during the eightees. The last ten years of the century saw a ferment of new ideas which gave birth to a fresh set of forces in the literary world. It witnessed a reaction against many old Victorean ideals. The new movement bears same resemblance to the romantic revival that quickened our sensibilities at the close of the 18th century, it is also effected by the revolutionary ideas of the age. Besides general resemblance there are particular differences that give it a distinctive character of its own.

The history of the 20th century English Literature is the literature of a vary complex age. It was the age of violence, upheavals and of great movement. The 20th century starts with the fine legacy of English novels. The 19th century was particularly rich in fiction. Starting with Jane Austen and Scot, it had such masters as Dickens. Thackerey, Meredith, George Eliott and Hardy.

Psychological interpretations were introduced in the II half of the 19th century. New light of the ideas were thrown by Henry James in the closing year of the last century. Emphasis was laid not on plot but on the character, the main attempt was to bring the inside out.

20th century opens with four outstanding novelists who more or less followed the traditional path. These four Arnold Benett, H.G. Wells, John Galsworthy and Joseph Conrad enriched the novel by their own social awareness and international feeling. Some new novelists of same promise also appeared on the scene. Somerset Mougham showed his power as a novelist but he had hardly anything new to say. E.M. Forster transferred the emphasis on plot to the novel. His novels are the novels of ideas.

Naturally there were the natural forces of revolt against the traditional novel. Freud exercised a strong influence. Freud's way attracted many young men and women. The outer world was disparaged and subjected inside because of the real domain of the artist. This diversion from the actual life, leads the artist sometimes to despair declaring the world and human life as meaningless, sometimes to the folds of religion and sometimes to the world of intellectual acrobatics.

New novelists in the decade were James Joyace, Virginia Woolf, Aldous Huxley and Richard Aldington. Forster and Lawrence added new treasure to English novel. Virginia Woolf had introduced a new kind, a new mode to English novel called the 'Stream of Consciousness'. She wants to discover the flew thing in life and the real thing for her was within the mind. Her attempt is therefore to reveal the flickering the inner most flame which flashes its message through the brain. The novel is hence known as the 'Stream of Consciousness Novel'. The writings of Richard Aldington and Aldous Huxlay had a bit of pessimism. Actually these writers were all escapist trying to run away from the challenges of life.

New voices were heard the other side of the Atlantic. It is significant that whereas in England, novelist, stood for negotiation of life, in America there was a call for acceptance and affirmation for life. Theodore Driser, Earnest Hamingway and John Stainback presented a life they saw it and they fell it and their faithful portrayal of life was appreciated everywhere. Man of other English novelists were holding the stage in the twenties and thirties of the century. The world during the last twenty years has undergone great changes and old values are all gone. The old institutions have virtually collapsed. Together with spectacular scientific advancement the weapons of mass destruction have also increased.

New forces for better life and better values have been certainly emerged but the forces of destruction with their nuclear weapon have also gathered in strength. The atmosphere is largely one of confusion, doubt and despair. Very few writers at present accept the challenges of their changed climate. Many of the the old guards are trying to weave out around them a web of escape and fantasy, as if nothing happened to the world, many are shelving the problems and would returning to solitude as if by that the problems would disappear. The new voices, the angry young man, protest against every established institution. They have no great ideals inspiring them, hence their protest are flatand have no significance.

The senior novelists except Joucecary have not produced anything of deep significance. Graham Green also to some extent maintains his power but he seems, too much obsessed with his particular themes. J. Comptton Burnett is happy with his upper middle class society of the Edwardian era. In total the novel was the most popular form of the literature in the 20th century. It has made various new experiments, it has discovered new world and new conquered different and unknown horizons. The novel in the present century is never stagnant, it is always moving.

The striking characteristic of the 20th century literature is extreme diversity. This diversity is only an aspect of wider heterogeneity in social development. The first half of this century witnessed World Wars which dealt a severe blow to the old values.

In a world where human values had brokendown and given place to scientific naturalism. It is perhaps worth mentioning here that new knowledge has always been accompanied by a crisis relating to the use of it. The new world appears to be increasingly incoherent and man, handicapped by his creation, is compelled to thrive in a state of deplorable helplessness.

The year 1890 may be regarded as a landmark in the literary and social history of England. It ushered in an era of rapid social changes, and this change is to be noticed in every sphere of life. By the last decades of the 19th century, there was a complete breakdown of the rural England had the increasingly urbanization of the country. Industrialization and urbanization brought new problems. The atmosphere has increasingly grown more and more smoky and noisy, city slums raise their ugly heads on all sides. By the end of 19th century and beginning of the 20th century, we find writers like Shaw, Wells and Galsworthy criticizing the very basis of the existing social, economical and moral system. In this atmosphere the philosophy of Freud dealt the situation more intricately. Freud emphasized the power of unconscious to effect conduct. Human being are not so rational as they are supposed to be; their conduct is not guided and controlled by the conscious. In this way a new dimension has been added to the assessment of human behaviour and more emphasis is being laid on the study of the unconscious. This has brought profound influence on 20th century moral attitude specially in matter of sex. Thus Freud and his followers have shown conclusively that repressed sex instincts are at the root of much neurotic and other signs of abnormality. His theory of 'Oedipus Complex' has caused a sensation and it is being freely exploited by 20th century writers. The study of sub-conscious, even the unconscious is the major theme of the modern literature. Intellect is no longer regarded as the means of true and real understanding, an emphasis is placed on feeling and intuition.

The Boer war (1899-1902) was a turning point in England's political life. The Boer war gave a rude shock to the complacent life and thinking of England. It revealed that the era of imperialism was to an end, and England had friends in Europe. Both the domestic and the foreign affairs, England was faced with grave problems. Indians under the able guidance of Gandhiji were demanding freedom from the British rule. T.S. Eliot's 'Waste Land' appeared as early as 1922 and the vision of twenties was created in the light of that poem which was rather a myth than the truth. Two years later the 'Waste Land' appeared Forster's 'A Passage to India'.

The greater mobility has also weakened the authority of old over the young and increased rootlessness of man. The rootlessness has brought in its wake its own problems and frustrations. Eliot's 'Waste Land' reveals a harrowing unconsciousness of this phenomenon of the 20th century city life. It may be called an era of revolt against authority. Political and religious scepticism general disillusionment, cynicism, irony, etc. have become the order of the day. Interest has shifted from the 'extrovest' to 'introvert'. There is an atmosprere of moral unease and uncertainly, a collapse of faith in the accepted pattern of social relationship and a search of new pattern.

The same perplexity and uncertainty is to be seen in political theory. Socialism and internationalism have replaced the old Victorian notions of supremacy of Whites. The disintegration of faith and traditional beliefs has led writers like D.H. Lawrence, to seek refuge from uncertainty and perplexity in some mystic religion of blood. Marxism has provided many with the vision of a new society which will replace the present one in not too distant future. Attention has been focussed on social, economical problems and planned development is favoured so that there may no extreme poverty side by side with great wealth. Thus the search for the 'system' and 'pattern' has resulted in the emergence of Marxism and the concept' of economic planning.

The modern age has witnessed a phenomenal rise in literacy. Cheap books, magazines and papers published in tones. However, these has been a visible decline in quality. The old culture of the people expressed in folk songs, dance, rustic craft etc., has been destroyed. The cinema, radio the popular literature full of stories and crime have exploited the people for commercial purpose. There has been an increase in vulgarity, brutality and coarseness. The exploitation of youth for commercial purpose assign to them a suspicious importance. It has become a century of the revolt of youth.

The one thing which stands out prominently in the history of English novel is its immense popularity at the turn of 19th century. It has eclipsed poetry and drama. It is the only literary from which has completed successfully with the radio and cinema, and it is in the genre that work of the greatest merit is being produced. This immense popularity may be accounted by the fact that modern man under the influence of science, requires discussions, clarification and analysis. This was possible only in novels, and hence the preference for it. Another prominent feature of the complexity. A number of different trends are to be noticed. There are the traditionalists like H.G. Wells, Arnold Beneh and Galsworthy who follow the Victorean tradition as far as the technique is concerned. On the other hand, there are innovators like Henry James, Joseph Conrad, James Joyce, Virginia, Woolf and E.M. Forster, have revolutionized the technique of the novel. Biographical, regional, satirical, sea, detective war and there are number of novels, continue to flood the market.

The modern novel is realistic. It deals with all the facts of contemporary life, the pleasant as well as the unpleasant, the beautiful as well as the ugly, and does not present merely the one sided view of life. The modern age is an era of disintegration, old values have been discarded and they have been replaced by new ones. The modern novel present realistically the doubts, the conflicts and the frustration of modern world. Joseph Conrad makes realism the basis of his romantic tales. E.M. Forster undisguised in his attack on the business mind and the worship of business in industrial England. Alduos Huxley analysis the disease of modern civilization. In modern novels there is no place for 'moralizing' and the dear reads. It is like a well out garden rather than a tropical jungle which Victorean novel was. For the Victorean novelist life easily fell into the mould of a story; but for the novelists of today, it refuses to do so. Moreover, it also embodies the writer's philosophy of Life, his massage and his view of human scene.

The modern novel is like an incomplete sentence and "its incompleteness is a reflection of incompleteness of a whole region of thought and belief". Under the influence of new psychological theory, life is not regarded as a continuous flow, but as series of successive moment.

Modern impact has been equally far reaching on the theme of the novel. The traditional novel was largely social, its being to uphold and reconcile social values. The theme of the modern novelist is not the relationship between gentility and morality but 'the novelist today is not concerned with 'the great society' which can be achieved only through great patience and care. Both Lawrence and Forster consider 'the great society' as enemy of the individual and want it to be reformed.

Such are the currents and the crass currents in the modern English novels. It is extremely vital and living form of art, and we can safely predict a bright and glorious future for it. Now influences specially the Russians and Americans are daily widening its horizons and renewing its vigour and vitality. New experiments are being conduct and the carvan of the English novel goes on, ever-changing, becoming and growing.

(B) Formative Influences & Forster's Development as a Novelist

"But when I die and they write my life they can write everything."

Foster to T.E. Lawrence
3rd May, 1928

E M. Forster is 'rare' because he is in part a late Victorean or an Edwardian and it is in part a modern. His life extends over a long period from 1879 to 1970 marked by rapid and radical social change. It is indeed difficult to find another British writer who has Forster's gift and whose relationship to the age covers such diverse phases of social and cultural changes for ninety years or more. However, it is not so much this uncommon relationship to the age that makes Forster so unique as the inherent qualities of his personality, mind and art.

Forster's relationship to his age is not quit a simple problem because the phases of that age are complex and the responses to them are varied. It extends from what Forster himself described as the 'fag-end of Victorean Liberalism', to the redical phase of present day Britain as a now socialistic welfare state.

What indeed is rare about E.M. Forster? J.R. Ackerley a close friend to Forster paid a glowing tribute to Forster by saying 'Forster is a very special man':

> "Few people can have had so many close affectionate friends as he had, and all of them, dead or alive, man or woman, youth or old, high or low, British or foreign will have regarded him as I did, as someone special, special to each of them."[1]

When Forster published the life of his friend Galsworthy Forster has commented on the difficulty of what he had been trying to do? If that was diffiault the uniqueness of Dickenson. If that was difficult the Dickenson's case it is still more so in his own. With Dickinson there was a golden thread running through everything he did and thought he had aligned himself with a particular tradition and his career was to be understood as a long attempt to remain true to the insight of that tradition.

Edward Morgan Forster was born at 8, Malcombe place, Dorset square, London on 1 January, 1879, to Alice Clara and Edward Morgan. His paternal and maternal heritage becomes the source of the Wilcoxes and the Schlegls in the 'Howards End'. Not long after Forster's birth, his father's health began to breakdown; he developed a chronic cough and was constantly catching colds, soon it was found that he was in advance stage of consumption; and by 30 Oct. 1880, he was dead. It left Forster's mother Lily grieving and bewildered and it seems that her only hope for future now lay with her baby. During the March of 1883 Lily and Forster moved into their new house. 'Rooksnest' in Stevengo, with which they both fell in love in no time at all. It is said that Forster evoked the house and his love for it in his novel 'Howards End.'

Forster became eleven in January 1890 and it was evidently high time for him to be at school. His mother investigated several pre-school and eventually selected 'Kent-House' in East Bourne. After his first week there was a reaction and he wrote home dispiritedly:

> "I have been to the baths and once and did not like or dislike them, when I got in a little way could not get my bath, after a few second I did not. I think I will tell you, I am not happy, what with the moving and other things it makes me feel bad. Please send another Bible take care of Kitty."[2]

By the time Forster had reached sixth at Cambridge. Much thought has been given to his career by an influential aunt. She took him for granted that he must go to be best college there. The choice fell on King's and in Christmas 1896, he took scholarship examination at King's college and though he failed to achieve an award, he secured a place in college. Forster entered King's College Cambridge in 1897 and was pleasantly surprised by the cordiality and intellectual playfulness of that enchanting institution. It was common for men to fell in love with Oxford and Cambridge. Forster did so too. Cambridge transformed him and he always acknowledged the debt. Forster's view of Cambridge, specially King's, expresses his deep personal involvement and his total identification with it. His altitude is also in keeping with his humane and liberal outlook. Forster writes with deep feeling and affection.

Forster entered King's College, Cambridge, in the autumn of 1897 and he remained there till 1901. His experience at Cambridge was just the reverse of his Tonbridge experience Cambridge suggested a new way of life which was based on leisure, freedom, friendship and personal relationships. The Cambridge of the 'Eighties' and of the 'Nineties consisted of men who, according to Goldsworthy' Lowes Dickinson, were "unworldly without being saintly" and "sceptical without being paralysed."[3] E.M. Forester, Lytton Strachey and J.M. Keynes were considerably junior to Bertrand Russell. They enjoyed life thoroughly for they had "Lots of fun" Bertrand Russell, in his book 'Portraits from Memory and other Essays', recalls the days of his youth and writes:

> "It was Generation that
> I am glad to have belonged to".[4]

At Cambridge, Forster discovered the non-existence of formality of any kind. The nerve center of Cambridge was the "Apostles". The Cambridge society was an exclusive group of intimate friends whose discussions were lively, critical, dispassionate and free from rancour and dogmatism. It encourage the young man to seek truth rather than victory. When its influence went wrong, it lad one to "self-consciousness and superciliousness". When its influence was in the right direction as in the case of Forster, it led to sharpness of mind. According to G.M. Trevelyan, the critical atmosphere prevailing in Cambridge was "an astringent" that served him well and "his natural tendency to be hasty and superficial was kept constantly under correction".[5] Forster imbibed the "spiritual culture" of Cambridge rather than its "snobbish esteem" and its pride in "intellectual culture".[6] Forster was happy at Cambridge which was a place "for the very young and the very old". Obviously, Forster disliked self-consciousness, intellectual arrogance and pride. Cambridge, the supreme symbol of "sweetness and light", hypnotized Forster by "the spirit that is genuine and likely and cultured and playful", Cambridge, according to Goldsworthy Lowes Dickinson, suggested fusion. King's college, however, suggested to Forster, according to K.W. Gransden, his own view of the "muddle and mystery" of life.[7] Forster came under the influence of his classics tutor Nathaniel Wedd. The study of the classics, according to K.W. Gransden, reveals to Forster the Greek view of life and art—"the classical division of man into the rational part and the animal part".[8] Dr. Leavis, while reviewing Lionel Trilling's book—E.M. Forster—A Study—is critical of Forster's vision of Cambridge as presented by him in The Longest Journey and also of Trilling's view.[9] Dr. Leavis comments:

> "But surely, what a critic who takes Forster seriously must be very largely concerned with nowadays is how that university did equip him—to deal with the milieu into which it sent him the milieu, so closely connected with Cambridge, that became Bloomsbury?"[10]

The six members of the mid-night society, the core of the Bloomsbury Group, were Saxon Sydney-Turner, Leonard Woolf, Lytton Strachey, Thoby Stephen, A.J. Robertson and Clive Bell. The members of the Bloomsbury group, like the claphamites, criticized each other unsparingly but with affection. Bloomsbury admitted only those members who hold liberal views and showed shear contempt for dogmatism in religion and conservatism in polities. Its philosophy was rational and sceptical because it rejected dogma and discarded the supernatural part of Christianity which is considered as 'hocus-pocus'.[11] It was opposed to utilitarianism and totally discarded the practical philosophy of self-interest and success. Bloomsbury neo-aestheticism was altogether unworldly and marked the beginning of a new renaissance: "Our religion was altogether unworldly—with wealth, power, popularity or success it had no concern whatever, they were thoroughly despised".[12] Bloomsbury stressed the importance of tolerance in matters of sexual mores, aesthetic pursuits, personal relationships, the life of passionate contemplation, need for spirituality and truthfulness to one's emotions. Bloomsbury, in the opinion of Stephen Spender, represented certain attitudes which almost became a cult. One could belong to it provided one was an agnostic in religion and "a Liberal" in politics. E.M. Forster was "impish", T.S. Eliot was "dogmatic".

"For this reason Eliot was too dogmatic in religion and too conservative in politics to fit in. It is more difficult to say why Forster does not quite fit. He was perhaps too impish, too mystical too moralizing."[13]

E.M. Forster and T.S. Eliot were associated with Bloomsbury rather than "belonging" to it. The positive qualities of Bloomsbury reason and intelligence, sanity and decency culture and enlightenment, tolerance and good will, leisure and pleasure, reading and learning, thinking and good living were shared not only by Forster and Eliot, but by nearly all the best talent of this period.[14]

Bloomsbury's sense of humour was highly developed; according to Noel Annan, it was gay, satirical, and ironic. No wonder, the scepticism of Forster and his friends came "not from personal experiences of disillusion but from a legacy which they accepted with varying degree of earnestness". Bloomsbury had no respect for convention and traditional standards.[15]

Forster visited Greece and Italy in 1901 and he return in home 1902. It was the Mediterranean world which opened his eyes to beauty; the contemplative peace of rustic life, the simple joy of life lived at low tension, the health giving vitality of natural surroundings, and the instinctive life which is a mean of escape from the "surroundings and decadehce" of the industrial civilization of modern times. The Mediterranean civilization suggested to Forster the elemental forces—Pan, Ceres, Demeter and Artemis—such as of brutality, vitality, and fertility. In an age of materialism, the pagan outlook of Forster was a necessary corrective to the bourgeois outlook. The Hellenism of Forster in his short stories is primarily instinctual. Shoddy values of the urban civilization. Forster benefitted from his Greek experience which revealed to him the importance of an integrated personality, of common humanity, of a quiet life of nature, and of the passion for truth.

Greek suggested to Forster the natural world of Pan and the Faun. Italy, on the other hand suggested the "outer world of spontaneous and joyful living".[16] Italy in fact was the very antithesis of Sawston. Samuel Butler, Alps and Sanctuaries, has given a detailed description of northern Italy and the Pagan outlook of the Italian peasantry. He loved the Italian peasants for their child like playfulness, self-abandonment, spontaneity of feeling, and hearty enjoyment of life. Samuel Butler and Forster are a like in their admiration of the natural qualities displayed by the Italian peasants. They loved the Italians for their pagan outlook, for their hatred of cant and phlegm, for their disapproval of intellect, for their love of music, and for their zest for the natural life. Samuel Butler and Forster advocate "the interfusion", into the English way of life or more of the Italian spirit. Forster's experience of life in the Mediterranean world stood in glaring contrast to his experience of life at Tonbridge school. Italy and Sawston suggest to Forster the two opposing pair's—candour and hypocrisy, truthfulness and falsehood, zest for life and phlegm, intuition and intellect, natural instincts and conventionality. Forster's visit to Greece and Italy was fruitful for he returned home with the two living symbols of "truth" and passion".[17] The vision of the classical world which Forster attributes to Gemistus Pletho, "the Renaissance Greek who loved the pagan gods and did his part in the revival of Greek learning in Italy",[18] is in fact, the vision of the earlier Forster. The 'hellenism' of Forster's earlier work was of "the simple idealising sort"—a nostalgia for blessed simplicity and a plea for the natural life—while the 'hellenism' of the Forster implies a "recognition and acceptance of complexity".[19]

Forster's association with India began long before he ever went to India. He made Indian friends in England. Forster met Syed Ross Masood in 1977 and he became one of his closest friends. His first visit to India was made in 1912-1913 with Goldsworthy Lowes Dickinson. This visit Forster calls "a Muslim visit," for he stayed with Syed Ross Masood. It is interesting to note the impressions of Dickinson and Forster about India. Dickinson saw the important sights of India in about three months but he felt "suffocated". Indian art, Indian religion, and Indian society were quite alien to him. For the Anglo-Indians, however, Dickinson felt a sympathy "tinged with a kind of despair" "the more conscientiously they did their work further they were from the native sympathy and mind" Forster's second visit, "a Hindu visit",[20] was made in 1921. He worked as private secretary to the Maharajah of Dewas senior. This visit was most interesting and unusual and he has written about it in 'The Hill of Devi'. Forster's third visit the"national visit," was made in 1945 when he went out to attend a conference of the "P.E.N. All-India Group" at Jaipur. Forster spokes about "The necessity of form in literature and the importance of the individual vision".[21] India, it seems, enlarged the vision of Forster, sensitized his mind, performed the "couching operation", and enabled him to see life in a new perspective. In 'Pan' Forster writes' that the East is "mysterious enough, mysterious to boring point.[22] Forster knows that human nature is the same everywhere and cannot be altered. His ironic vision destructs the "mysterious" and is fully aware of both the comic and the tragic aspects of human life. Forster was aware of the political situaticn in India and he was also conscious of the racial question which was delicate. In the city of Jodhpur, according to Forster, the 'racial question' had been solved the English and the Indians shared the same club:

> "It was as if each race had made concessions. Ours seemed more sensitive then usual, the Indian more solid. A common ground for friendship had been contrived...[23]

India, indeed, "Added a dimension to Forster as a creative artist".[24] It, perhaps, added a new concepts of life which was different from his "liberal-bourgeois-agnostic" mind. India, it appears, seems to have conceived him of the weakness of personal relationship, of the dangers of liberalism, of the limits of rationalism, of the emptiness of civilization, of smallness of the globe, and of the indifference of the universe to human life.

Forster's own experience at home and abroad, his observance of Suburbia and the country life, and his own contemplative vision contributed to the growth of his mind. His bourgeois upbringing give him "a middle-class slant" upon life which was corrected by contact with friends and also by his own observation and experience of life. Tonbridge, the "Sawston" of his novels, developed his dislike of the public-school system which turns out men with "undeveloped hearts". Cambridge suggested to Forster sweet reasonableness and the civilized way of life. Forster came under the influence of his friend Goldsworthy Lowes Dickinson who loved music, books, and scenes and believed "reason, integrity, tolerance, compassion, love and art".[25] Forster, like Goldsworthy Lowes Dickinson, protest against the emptiness of the modern world and lays stress upon personal relationship, love, toleration and the inner life. McTaggart taught his generation the importance of the winding power of love, the illusory nature of time and space and the possibility of eternal life and perfection. Forster's liberalism, individualism, and agnosticism are "attitudes". Forster is critical to the Clopham Sect:

> "Solidly religious, they give one the impression of having no sense whatever of the unseen."[26]

This indifference to the unseen was a great defect in the religious faith of the Clapham Sect. "Poetry, mystry, passion, ecstasy, music" were not important to them. Forster likes the Quakers because they have what the Claphamites lacked: "a touch of mysticism, a sense of the unseen and a capacity for martyrdom.[27] Thus Forster's own sense of "religiosity" is clear from his attitude towards the unseen life. In his novels, Forster values personal relationship, toleration, good will, freedom of the human spirit, and all these human values which have been cherished by mankind from time immemorial.

Keeping himself aloof from the human tangle, Forster observed the co-existence of triviality and profoundity in life. He saw life critically and dispassionately and conveyed his unified vision of society and the individual in his novels. Disgusted with the respectability of the middle-class, the class-consciousness and snobbery of the upper middle-class, the arrogance of the official, the hypocrisy of the priestly class and the tyranny of institutions, he sought relief and found it in his true self.

After the death of his mother in 1945 Forster was unable to retain ownership of his beloved house at 'Abinger' in Surray.

The problem of where to live was solved by the King's cottage Cambridge, elected him as honorary fellow and then according him the rare additional privilege to residing there. When India's independence came on 15th August, 1947, Forster gave broadcast on the SSC Eastern service entitled" Massage to India." By 1953, he was the grand old man of letters and having completed "The Hill of Devi" had set to work upon the fourfold biography of his aunt "Marianne Thornton".

Forster was an active writer and influenced very much till to end of 1950. In April 1961, a few month letter Ackerley's, his friend and writer, return to Japan, Forster visited him in flat at Putney and had a fall on a threshold, breaking his wrist and suffering shock. Ackerley said— 'No one else had ever done it in a grumbling tone but Morgan choose it'. Meanwhile Forster collapsed one more and had been rushed in to a hospital. He was suffering from a blood deficiency and for a day or two before this was diagnosed, his life was in danger. Later in his common place book he recorded the experience which he had confirmed him in his belief that death if you can approach it as search:.

> "No pain, no fear, no though, no eternity, fate, love, humanity or any of the usual weakness and too weak to be aware of anything to be weak."[28]

E.M. Forster is one of the most controversial figures of the 20th country fiction. It is difficult to assess his real place. Walter Allen remarks:

> "Forster as a novelist—is difficult to assess his real place in the history of 20th century fiction. He can be as easily overestimated as underestimated."[29]

There are critics who regarded him as the father of

modern English novel. But at the same time, there are some critics who find his writings something dull. Virginia Woolf observes:

> "Forster is in any case an author about whom there is considerable disagreement. There are something baffling and evasive in the very nature of his gift."[30]

Forster became popular at the outset of his career as a novelist in 1950s. In the half of the century his literary pilgrimage, Forster wrote sixteen books, five novels, two volumes of short stories, two volumes of critical essays, travel books and pamphlets. In this way Lionall Trilling writes:

> "There is different of opinion about his talent, Forster is the only living novelist who can be real again and again and who gives a sensation to the readers."[31]

Forster gives the two name to his reality, fantasy and prophesy. Fantasy involves the use of mythological gods of ship of memory. The novelist is likely to use this purpose such add device like angels for this ghost or a monkey all in order to make us accept either the supernatural or its absence. Prophesy according to Forster has a mythology that suggests unity a mingling of physical reality with some universal or something universal, though it does not necessarily say something about it. Fanlasy like prophesy is one of the aspects of the novel discussed by Forster while discussing the story as the fundamental aspect of the novel, he wishes that the novel should be 'something different' melody or the perception of the truth. Melody is selected to the rhythrn, but the fantasy and prophesy are the ways of perceiving the truth, fantasy is therefore, a device of narrative. C.S. Lewis defines it as a "Narrative that deals with the impossible and preternatural".[32]

Forster says that a novel has both human beings and a bundle of various things fantasy is concerned with those which are not human beings. Even the extraordinary or super human behaviour of the human beings are subjects of fantasy.

As fantasy is improbable, marvellous and extraordinary, some extra attention is needed to grasp them.

E.M. Forster mixes fantasy in the narrative of the stories and novels to view reality in relation to myth, supernatural elements and a living past. By doing so he present a reality which incomprehensible to the intellect. Fantasy adds symbolism to the structure of the novel. This attains different layers of meaning when the novelist weaves the incidents, with myth symbols, supernatural and the living places. The use of fantasy is fictional. Forster says that one caution needed by the writers of fantasies is that they should not be incredible. They must carry the readers.

The use of fantasy in the novel gives a sudden jolt and pushes the readers in to a new awareness of the double vision of this world and of a world where myth seems real, places are alive and the people attain uncommon powers and create extraordinary situation. Fantasy is a foil to reality to highlight and study it in depth. It is a device of using something strange, unreal and supernatural or even absurd to study the complex, multi dimensional and mysterious human reality. It inlarges the range of experience. It is through fantasy that the reality can be really exposed.

There are the two common ways to introduce fantasy in the novel explicit and implicit: Forster's own novels are illuminating illustrations of both expressed and implied fantasy. The behaviour of Gino, Mrs. Moore, Mrs. Wilcox cannot be judged as normal features of life. Even places in his novels attain supernatural powers. They have a spirit. They are the actors and measure the human sensibility. Austen Warran's, observation on Forster's use of fantasy is very illuminating.

"The element of fantasy, with Forster in conveyed not through a mechanism but through a colouring: ordinary existence is illuminated by the white, light of eternity of the blue light of 'value', so that the familiar landscape gains on arresting strangeness".[33]

If we examine fantasy as a technique in Forster's novels, we find three main forms: Myth, Place and People. Forster uses them as a technique of revealing the hidden area of human experiences. Forster's fantasy is not a technique of escape but a complex device of presenting the reality of life and society. He uses fantasy to enrich the symbolic aspect of the novel and to add an allegorical dimension to it. It is like a boring machine that cuts across the layers of consciousness to reach the deeper and deeper springs of life.

Pattern and system which Forster discuss next belong to the aesthetic aspect of the novel. As to the pattern, he discusses the ways through which the variety in experiences can be given an adequate shape. He favours a pattern which is most closely in touch with its material. The pattern is closely related to the plot and is woven with characters and scenes. The theme and the pattern are interlinked and indivisible. An appreciation of pattern is also an appreciation of the subject matter. Forster's metaphor a light in the cloud' hints at the aesthetic aspect of the pattern. Similarly the pattern in the novel should cross and illuminate characters, scenes and incidents. It unites experiences into a single aesthetic whole. Unity is itself beautiful. Beauty is an essential aspect of the pattern but it should not be captured. Because as Arnold Kettle says that pattern is the way, life develops.

Forster's theory of rhythm in the novel shows his dissatisfaction with the traditional concept of pattern on the one hand, and on the other, his consistent endeavour to explore a language which can be a reflection of the rhythm in his life. His search for rhythm in the novel is a search for a better form than pattern. For him rhythm is more powerful, more expensive and more persuasive than any form or structure.

Forster's view on rhythm are very important to the world of theory and criticism of novels. He was the only artist who find the future of rhythm and music in fiction. His novels are shows that novel is akin to music. His novels are the wonderful illustrations of the analogy of music and fiction. In 'Aspect of the Novel'. He says:

> "Music and rhythm is the essential part of the novel. In music, fiction is likely to find its nearest parallel".[34]

Grouping and regrouping of characters, various contrasts of events and people, and interrelatedness of various events and section add a rhythmical structure to novel. Forster is aware of the difficulty of a novelist who wants to give a musical shape to his novels, but he is of the opinion that a novel can attain the shape of music. He says:

> "Music though it does not employ human beings, though it is governed by the intricate laws, nevertheless does offer in its final expressions a type of beauty which fiction might achieve in its own way."[35]

Rhythm, as Forster points out, is essential to explain the meaning and to evolve a form, a harmony ana an order form within. When music starts, it grows through various contrasted tunes suggesting various feelings, but there is an order within. Similarly in novels rhythm emerges from repetitions and contrasts, divisions and differences, in which there is a unique internal harmony. Rhythm comes out from the structure of events in the novel but it also shapes the structure. Both are indivisible like blood and flesh. He does not define rhythm but what he means by it is well explained in his observation of two types of rhythm.

"Rhythm is sometimes quite easy. Beethoven's fifth symphony, for instance, starts with the rhythm; 'diddidy dum', which we can all hears and tap to. But the symphony as a whole has also a rhythm—due mainly to the relation between its movement—which some people can hear but no one can tap to. This second sort of rhythm is difficult and whether it is substantially the same as the first sort only musician could tell us.

A good rhythm in the novel is that which carries within the meaning. A well laboured rhythm is boring. It is a bridge that unites the world with vision. If the rhythm is used well, it leads us to the fuller awareness of the text of the novel and to the center of its meaning.

Forster is also the satirist and critic of society of the contemporary civilization based on the ideals of the materialism and money worship. Forster satirizes the material craze of the Wilcoxes of our society. He castigates the snobbery of highly placed persons like Henery and Charles Wilcox in "Howards End", Mr. and Mrs. Harriet in "Where Angels Fear to Tread", and Agnes Pembroke in "The Longest Journey". He has no sympathy for those whose hearts and souls have been sacrificed at the alter of the worldly success. Sometimes the attack is implicit but mostly it is explicit. A.C.Ward remarks:

> "His satires are sharp and penetrating as he deals with conventions and incidents, and there is profound irony in the poising of massive effects upon tiny causes, like a monster's inverted pyramid."[36]

Forster believed in love, tolerance, friendship and in affection. His circle of friends was very wide and it transcended national and linguistic barriers. E.M. Forster was a very special and rare man because he represented all that was best in the old world of late Victorian and Edwardian England. His charm, kindness, generosity, his saintliness were rare in their own way. His letters and brief notes, reflecting the magic of his personality, rare evidence of his large heartedness as well as his hard core compromising value on which he would not compromising at all. Arnold Kettle remarks:

> "He is not a writer of the stature of D.H. Lawrence or Joyce, but he is a fine and enduring artist and the only British novelist who can be discussed without any doubt against the highest and broadest standard."[37]

Forster was not an idle observer of his age but a keen interpreter of it. He had a vast experience of travel. This helped him in entering into the common experience of his generation. He grasped what was important in the thought of his age and did not grapple with it. It was his time that had played a vital role in making his mind. Forster's literary career cover the first quarter of the 20th century. Rarely has any period held such complexity and contradiction, such progress and such retrogression, such marvels and such futility as the age of Forster holds for the student of life and letters.

In November 1964, Forster had a wild stroke in Cambridge and he was left for a week or two week with stirred speech and difficulty in writing on his 90th birthday. Forster was presented a copy bounded in leather of 'Aspect of E.M. Forster' by Vice-President Edward while on Friday 22th May, 1970. Forster had a final stroke and he was helpless having lost of the use of both of legs. He died without recovering consciousness early next morning. He died leaving instruction that he was to be disposed of whereever he happened to be at the time of his death and without religious observance.

Forster's overall achievement has to be estimated in terms that are not strictly aesthetic or technical. His books are filled with a passion for truth, in personal emotions and relationship, a hatred for what is false and complacent. He excepts the size and grandeur of the world and then comes to grip with it with a vigorous modesty. Add to his positive sense of culture and awareness of its significance for the individual, his concerns, in fact, with the social dimension on a world scale. The outcome is a world of art which in its shape alters what exists.

His place in modern fiction is pretty high, for he is a novelist who raises his voice against modern materialism and advocates cultural values in a world overridden by philistines and Wilcoxes. His insistence of personal relationship, sweet reasonableness and tolerance have made him the messenger of peace. From the technical point of view, his novels provide a rich feast satisfying our poetical, aesthetic, moral, satirical sensibilities. There is rich variety of his novels, and it is the varied tastes that he satisfies which have made the favourite of many readers. He is right to say himself the fag end of Victorian Liberalism.

References

1. Ackerley, Jr. " Morgan: A Personl Memoir", The Observed (London, 1970), p. 7.
2. Furbenk, P.N., " E.M. Forster – A Life" . Oxford Univ. Press (London 1979), p. 33.
3. Dickinson, G.L., Quoted by Neol Annan in Leslie Stephen (London 1951), p. 286.
4. Russel, Betrand, Portrait from Memory and Other Essays (London 1956) p. 70.
5. Trevelyan, G.M., "An Autobiography and Other Essays" (London 1949) p. 14.
6. Swinnerton, Frank, "The Georgian Literary Scene" (No. 9430f Everyman's Library, London, 1938), p. 287.
7. Gransden K.W., "E.M. Forster" (London, 1962), p. 6.
8. *Ibid.,* p. 79.
9. Leavis, F.R., Review of Trilling's E.M. Forster – A Study (Scrutiny, Vol. XII, 1944-45, Cambridge University Press, 1963), p. 308.
10. *Ibid.,* p. 308.
11. Keynes, J.M. : My Early Beliefs, Two Memoirs (London 1949), p. 96.
12. *Ibid.,* p. 84.
13. Spender Stephan, World Within World (London, 1951), p. 140.
14. *Ibid.,* pp. 140-141.
15. Crews, Frederick C., "E.M. Forster: The Perils of Humanism" (Princeton University Press, 1962), p. 10.
16. Holt, Lee Elbert, E.M. Forster and Samuel Butter (P.M.L.A. XI, Sep. 1946), p. 806.
17. Trilling, Lionel, E.M. Forster – A Study (London, 1944), p. 34.
18. *Ibid.,* p. 33.
19. Kingopulos, G.D. E.M. Forster's sense of History – Essays in Criticism, Vol. VIII, (Oxford, April, 1958), p. 162.
20. Hasan, Aley. "The Life and Thought of E.M. Forster", The Sunday Standard, New Delhi, Dec. 11, 1960.

21. Forster, E.M., "Two Cheers for Democracy" India Again, p. 329.
22. Forster, E.M., "Abinger Harvest" 'Pan', p. 358.
23. Forster, E.M., "Abinger Harvest", Jodhpur, p. 346.
24. Gransden, K.W., "E.M. Forster" (London, 1962), p. 82.
25. Dickinson, G.L. "Letters from John Chinaman" (with an introduction by E.M. Forster), 1901, (London, Rep. 1948), p. 7.
26. Forster, E.M., "Abinger Harvest", 'Battersea Rise', p. 281.
27. Forster, E.M., "Two cheers for Democracy", Henry Thornton, p. 200.
28. Furbank, P.N. "E.M. Forster – A Life", Oxford University Press (London, 1979), p. 315.
29. Allen, Walter: "The English Novel", London, Phoeni House, 1954. p. 243.
30. Woolf, Virginia: "The Novels of E.M. Forster", The Death of Moth & Other Essays, New York, Harcourt Brace & Co. 1942. p. 161.
31. Trilling, Lionall "E.M. Forster – A Study", London, Hogarth Press, 1943, p. 42.
32. Lewis, C.S., "An Experiment in Criticism" Cambridge Univ. Press, 1965, p. 50.
33. Warrens, Austen: "The Theory of Literature" 1901-1940. Methuen & Co. Ltd. Land, 36 Essex Street Stand W.E.Z. 1953.
34. Forster, E.M. "Aspect of the Novel", London, Edward Arnold, 1927, p. 169.
35. *Ibid.,* p. 170.
36. Ward, A. C., "20th Century Literature" 1901-40 London, Methaen & Co. Ltd., p. 242.
37. Kettle, Arnold, "An Introduction to the English Novel", Vol.2 (London Mutchinson Univ. Press, Library 1953), p. 132.

2

Different Themes in the Novels of E.M. Forster

> "I know that the personal relations are the real thing"
> E. M. Forster in Howard's End.

E. M. Forster's all five novels is actually a very important document in the study of human relationship. F. R. Leavis rightly calls him, "pre-eminently a novelist of civilized personal relation ."[1] Margaret Schlegal one of the leading character of his novel "Howard's End" says:

> "I've often thought about it, Helen. It is one of the most important thing in the world. The truth is that there is a great outer life that you and I have never touched a life in which telegram and anger count. Personal relation, that we think supreme, are not supreme there. Their love means marriage settlements, death, death duties. So far I am clear. But here is my difficulty. This outer life though obviously horrid, often seems the real one—there's girl in it. It does breed character; Do personal relations lead to sloppiness in the end?"[2].

Forster's ideology about the creed of personal relations not merely depends in heart's affection and all goodness in the men. Forster does not believe that the .world is a globe of men who are trying to reach one another and can best do so with the help of goodwill plus culture and intelligence. In fact Forster's creed of personal relations is very complex: While he believes in the value and essentiality of personal relations he also knows that human relationship is always breaking down for some reason or the other. Sometimes it even seems to him that there is at best only a limited value to be derived from personal relationships alone.

In his earlier novels, Forster is primarily concerned with matters of human conduct and especially with the dark places in the human heart which make for unhappiness and confusion not only between individuals but between the races and nations.

"Passage to you, your shores ye aged fierce enigmas! Passage to you to mastership of your, ye strangling problems!

You strewed with the wrecks of skeletons that living never reached you."[3]

E.M. Forster had a very set idea about the existence of the personal relations. As he was a liberal so his philosophy about the ideas of liberal tradition very closely mingled with the human relationship. He is not blind to the inadequacies of personal relations. Adela's Marabar experience makes her redlies the inadequacy of warmth and love:

> "What is the use of, personal relationship when everyone bring less and less to them? I feel we ought all to go back into the desert for centuries and try and get good. I want to begin at the beginning. All the things thought I'd learnt are just a hindrance. They are not knowledge at all. I am not fit for personal relationship."[4]

In the earlier part of his novels Forster expresses his unshakable belief in the possibility of communication between individuals. Aziz and Indian Muslim and Mrs. Moore an old Englishwoman, meet in a mosque and achieve a "secret understanding of the heart." When they come to the mosque both of them have wanted to escape from the oppressive atmosphere created by British in Chandrapore. Aziz has been snubbed contemptuously by the British and has come miserable and hurt, to the mosque "Shaking the dust of Anglo-India off his feet." Mrs. Moore also has escaped from the English club, bored by the tedious play being staged there and has come to the mosque to seek place and relief. The mosque with its quit beauty, it's tight and shade, represent a belief in the oneness of India and also a understanding among people. Mrs. Moore is kindly an old woman, who is full of love and sympathy for Indian's, unlike her fellow Britishers who consider Indians as belonging to an inferior race and therefore not fit to establish personal relationship with Mrs. Moore, as Aziz says of her, is almost oriental in her broad sympathies and she responds with kindness and understanding to Aziz's complaints against the British. The aggrieved Aziz is soothed by the kindness and simplicity of a warmhearted British woman. There develops between these two dissimilar people a warm bond of understanding which survives many strains racial and otherwise—imposed one it.

Dr. Aziz represents the sincerely and warm heartedness of India, and when he found the Britishers totally dejected he feels in-comfort among them, but it was Mrs. Moore's affection and sensitivity which blows a kind of fragrance between them. Their voyage for spirituality comes to an end in the mosque, and by their union they know the two symbol of India's secret understanding of the heart and sacrifice. Their friendship is not a traditional kind but they represent the two important aspect of life. Dr. Aziz represents the sincere and intellectual Indian people, who is very much engaged in public affairs, and Mrs. Moore a cultured English woman represents the true tenderness and affection to the Indians as the Britishers do not treating the Indians in the civilized manner.

The most important relationship taken by the Forster in 'A Passage to India' is that of Dr. Aziz and Fielding. Dr. Aziz is a doctor in Minto Hospital run under the supervision of an English surgeon, Major Calendar. Fielding is the principal of Govt. College of Chandrapore. By birth he is English. This relationship in the novel is developed as a representative Anglo-India relationship. Both of them are intimate friends. Forster shows how goodwill and spontaneity bridge the deep gulfs between people of different races. Aziz's impulsiveness and Fielding's friendliness dissolve the racial barriers between them. When they meet in first time in Fielding's house, one notices the contrast between them: the easy going Englishman 'travelling light' and the young Muslim 'Placed, placed routed in society and Islam'. Aziz is impulsive, easily given to love and hate, sensitive to the slightest reactions of his British rulers towards him and yet desperately wanting to be liked by them. Fielding on the other is a mature, genial liberal, free from race, feeling and remaining tolerant and detached in a land which demands the fiercest loyalties to the natives or to the British as the case may be. Yet all these differences are at first dissolved by their mutual trust in each other and the power affectionate friendship. Fielding has the genuine feeling to Dr. Aziz. It is he who opposes the step taken by the society and authorities against Aziz. He regards him as innocent. He resigns from the membership of the club, and has to bear insult and hate from his own race. Even then he supports Dr. Aziz in this trial. He is ready to resign his post and leave India if Dr. Aziz is termed guilty by the court of law. If his through his actions that we are made to believe for some time that it is possible to be friend with the English. But later on at Mau forest, we find that this relationship collapses as a wall of sand. The quarrel arises out of Aziz's criticism of the British rule. Fielding can't tolerate all this and Dr. Aziz cries out.

> "Clear out, all you Turtons and Burtons. We wanted to know you ten years back now its too late. If we see you and sit on your committees, its for political reason" don't you make any mistake."[5]

He goes on adding:

> "Clear out, Clear out, I say. Why are we put to so much suffering? We used to blame you, now we blame ourselves, we grow wiser. Until England is in difficulties we keep silent, but in the next European war -aha, aha! Then is our time."[6]

Fielding mocked again. And Aziz is an awful rage danced this way and that, not knowing what to do, and cried Down with this English anyhow. That certain.

But this was not a miracle that they have break their relationship and friendship. They belong to two totally different society and culture. While Aziz was over sensitive and frustrated that Britishers were not good in behaviour with the Indians. He was actually a strong criticizer of British rule in India. He suffered a lot by the behaviour of Mr. Calendar and his wife. The ugly manner of Ronny and the disguising blame of Adela. Fielding was very much familiar with these things but he could give only moral support to Aziz, as he was also a Britisher. Even in the first meeting between them, there are hints that Fielding's undeveloped imagination and Aziz over-sensitive imagination are going to bode ill for their future relationship. Later when they are again drawn to each other and Aziz, in a moving gesture of friendship, shows Fielding his dead wife's photograph, we are made aware of differences in character and outlook between them. Fielding is slightly put off by this gesture: he can't be carried away on waves of emotions as Aziz can. Misunderstanding finally arises between them in their attitude towards woman and even leads to their break after Aziz's release when Fielding asks Aziz to withdraw his revengeful demand for heavy damages from Adela Quested. They separate and when they reunite at the end, their characters and waves of life have changed radically. Fielding siding with Anglo-India and Aziz with Indian nationalism and they are unable to continue as close friend.

The course of Aziz-Fielding relationship points to the difficulties of men of difference races trying to understand one another. In the novel, Forster continually makes aware of the fact that relationship are always in the danger of breakdown. Nót only this, Forster wants to show us that there are limits to human communication: "What is the use of personal relationships when everyone brings less and less to them."

The friendship between Fielding and Adela reveals the limitations of a search for more personal relationship the inability to form deeper, more permanent relations, to surrender to anything outside the self, the lack of imagination to understand experiences that cannot be understood in terms of reason and so on. Both Fielding and Adela exemplify these emotional and imaginative limitations. In their last meeting, Fielding and Adela talk about the experiences that have made them what they are. Both have become wiser after the incident at the caves and they are now willing to accept the mystery of the caves, instead of finding a rational explanation for it. But in spite of their greater awareness, Forster tell us in a crucial passage about their inability to grasp imaginative experiences that. beyond their rational consciousness:

> "A friendliness as of dwarfs shaking hand, was in the air. Both man and woman were at the height of their powers-sensible, and even subtle. They spoke the same language, and held the same opinions, and the variety of age and sex did not divide them yet they were dissatisfied. When they agreed 'I want to go on living a bit; or 'I don't believe in God', the words were followed by a curious backwash as though the universe had displaced itself to fill up a tiny void, or as though they had seen their own gestures from an immense height-dwarfs talking, shaking hands and assuring each other that they stood on the same footing of insight".[7]

Nirad Chowdhary in his article entitled "A Passage to and from India" attacks the description of personal relationships between British and Indians:

> "The great Indians who brought about the Westernisation of their country and created its modern culture and none of the characteristic Indian foibles for which Mr. Forster Invokes British compassion. They are the men of the stature of an Erasmus. Comenious, or Holdberg, who could hold their own with the best in Europe. Yet some of them were assaulted, some insulted, and other slighted by the local British."[8]

The basic idea which determines of the outer life to the life of the sprit, the rejection of conventions and business relationships, the preference of the little society, to the great society, the detestation of arrogant intellect, and the recognition of the claims of the heart. Forster's attitude towards life is, therefore quite clear from the basic idea which constitutes the theme of his novels, Agnus Wilson, in "An interview with E. M. Forster", writes: "Theme, he thought, came before plot "Everything in his novels seems to be directed and controlled by the shaping force of his imaginative vision which form the invincible center of his fiction. The vision of Forster is directed towards the basic theme of his novels. It is the "Burning core" that gives meaning to life; it is the "tender core of the heart "that creates personal relationships it is the 'sensitiveness of the soul' that responds to beauty and truth, and it is the true self of the man that is enduring. The basic theme of his novels centers round the living core of man and can be stated as the theme of truth, of personal relationship, of private life, of appearance and reality, and of society and self. Forster, in his novels, communicates his own vision of life—it is the vision of truth. Forster has cut himself off from the seeming life and Faith of his time, in order to discover truth.

The action of his novels is based upon the interaction of the opposing point of view. The conflict "between the conventional and the imaginative outlook, plays a part in all the novels."[9] By means of contrast, Forster succeeds in presenting a vision of life and the contrast he shows in his novels is the contrast which one can find in real life; It is the contrast between the real and the false. His novels, therefore, succeed in giving us the total impression of the life, his creative vision embraces the common place and the extraordinary, the pleasant and the unpleasant, the beautiful and the repulsive. Dorothy H. Heare has pointed out that the use of contrasting pairs of Forster's favourite method of indicating his own views:

> There is in his work an extremely subtle and constant juxtaposition of opposing value."[10]

Virgina Woolf, too has pointed out that antithesis is the indispensable focus of his novel:

> "Sawston implies Italy; timidity, wildness; convention, freedom; unreality, reality."[11]

The contrast between the two opposite modes of life has been worked out by Forster in his novels into diverse fictional forms-elaborate social comedy, fantasy and prophesy. The novels of Forster covers the whole gamut of life the Greek view of life, the medieval idea of asceticism, the renaissance concept of individuality, the eightieeth century and Victorian view of society, and the modern trend towards psychology. In 'Where Angles Fear to Tread' the contrast is between the pagan view and the conventional, in "A Room With a View", between medieval asceticism and the natural impulses; in "The Longest Journey" between reality and unreality; in "Howards End", between the outer life and the inner, in "A Passage to India", Forster deals with the great theme of art appearance and reality. What Forster has to say about Gide is, perhaps, true of Forster too:

> "...he had in many ways a pagan outlook, yet he had also a puritanical and religious outlook, which was inherent his upbringing and something dominated him."[12]

Forster is a writer whose books emphasize "the

importance of personal relationship.[13] The emotions which spring from the personal relationship are particularly important in as an age which is deficient in feeling. Forster believe that the emotions which spring from "the personal relation" are important in a world which, in the words of Mathew Arnold:

> "Hath really lither joy, nor love, nor light, nor certitude, nor peace, nor help for pain;"[14]

Forster's belief in personal relationships is "a legitimate literary theme."[15] Society provides no real basis for communication between individuals. In his personal relations, however, the individual's tender-heartedness come in. The individual needs not solitude but company, not self-sufficiency but love, not business relations but trust and warmth of affection. Forster criticizes South Hertfordshire, because it contains so many fenced—in gentlemen's parks. The first need in life is love:

> "That human being should be united with each other in love is to him the first need in life."[16]

In the private life, Forster finds solace:

> "Here is something comparatively solid in a world full of violence and cruelty."[17]

The private life is real:

> "It is the private life that holds out the mirror of infinity, personal intercourse, and that alone, that ever hints at a personality beyond our daily vision."[18]

The theme in "Where Angle Fear to Tread" is based on the clash of opposition forces and inner conflict of men, light and dearness, Italy and Sawston, the conventions of suburbia and the natural impulses of the natural man. According to William York Tindall, an oaf is used as a foil to the civilized:

> "The animal vitality of Carella in 'Where Angles Fears to Tread' quarrels with the deadness of the British suburb."[19]

The English middle-class virtues of respectability the repression of vigour, the cold act of charity, the high sense of duty, the exclusion of laughter, the rejection of beauty, and the lack of imagination loak foolish in the light of the sunny Italian temperament. Sawston is different from Italy:

> "Sawston was different: We had to keep up appearances."[20]

Forster shows his deep hatred of the English middle-class conventionality and his deep appreciation of the Itilion 'sweetness and barbarity'. Against the dull background of an English home with its atmosphere of 'morality and purity, and the holy life', Forster sets the Italian background of stars, sky, music, laughter, happiness and joy. 'Where Angels Fear to Tread' is a novel which deals with the vision of love and tenderness, of beauty and happiness, of out spoken frankness and sincerity of cheerfulness and the sense of religiousness, of joy and laughter, of pain and sorrow, of mens of life and vitality. The pleasant lision of beauty within and without, is contrasted with the unpleasant vision of dullness and triviality, of meanness and cruelty, of pride and selfishness, of morality and holiness, of stupidity and vulgarity, of hypocrisy and pretension, of pettiness and vice, the inner conflict of the people to achieve something noble. Even Miss Abbott has her moment of illumination when the scales of unreality fall from her eyes and she sees the essential goodness of Gino. Gino who teaches Philip the importance of physical love:

> "He had reached love by the spiritual path: her thought and goodness and her nobility had moved him first, and nowhere whole body and all its gestures had become transfigured by them."[21]

Philips eyes are opened by Gino who praises the beauties that are called 'obvious', "the beauties of her hair and her voice and her limbs," Miss Abbott reveals the vision of human suffering and she shows him the imperative need of love and compassion to mitigate pain:

> "Her eyes wlere open, full of infinite pity and full of majesty, as if they discerned the boundaries of sorrow, and saw unimaginable tracts beyond."[22]

Forster firmly believes that happiness is possible for man provided he has adequate imagination, sufficient insight, and self-awareness. Lee Elbert Holt rightly says that the principal theme of "Where Angles," is the "contrast between English hypocrisy and restraint and the open hearted self-conscious spontaneity of the Italian temperament."[23]

Forster moves from the pagan outlook in where Angle to the medieval view in 'A Room With a View.' The medieval view af life as based on the rejection of the body. Forster has stated that the medieval outlook was based on asceticism but in practice it led to sensuality, 'A Room With a View' is based on the theme of self-denial. The conventional people of English middle-class have an outlook which is characterized by the blindness of truth. Forster's sympathy are with the unconventional people who believe in the sanity of passion. Lucy Honeyehurch is awakened to love in the natural surroundings of Italy, but back in England she stifles the emotions of which the conventions and the world disapprove and is saved by Mr. Emerson who opens her inward eye to the reality of the love. The contest in "A Room With a View" is between two opposing pairs: the Greek view of life and the medieval outlook, fruition and celibacy, self-fulfillment and self-denial, bodily enjoyment and emotional starvation, light and darkness. The medieval theme is introduced by Rev. Cuthbert Eager, is associated with Cecil Vyse, and also with Mr. Beebe who, like St. Paul, believes in asceticism and in the freedom of the individual from the taint of sex. Mr. Beebe, like St. Paul believes in celibacy and chestity. Cecil Vyse believes in celibacy, and chivalry and he is the protector of the woman. He is happy when Lucy Honeyehurch refuses to marry him. Cecil Vyase an ideal bachelor, is medieval in his outlook. He is "in the grip of a certain devil whom the modern world knows as self-consciousness". He is medieval, and he suggests a gothic statue.

> "A Gothic statue implies celibacy, just as a Greek statue implies fruition, and perhaps this was what Mr. Beebe meant."[24]

These are three strands of the medieval spirit in the novel of courage and faith, of asceticism and purity, and of chivalry. Forster considers the Italians superior to the conventional English middle-class. The Italians, unlike the English, have geniality, grace sincerity and even brutality. Mr. Emerson the kind old man, enables Lucy "to see the light dancing in the Amo and the cypresses of San Miniato, and the foot-hills of the Apennines, black against the ıising moon."[25] Muddle is created by superstition and ignorance, and the only means of escape from the horror of life is love:

> "We know that we come from winds, and that we shall return to them; that all life is perhaps a tangle, a blemish in the eternal smoothness. But why should this make us unhappy? Let us rather love one another, and work and rejoice. I don't believe in this world sorrow."[26]

Mr. Emerson and George Emerson live in a room with a view. Cecil Vyse is connected not with an open view but with a drawing room. Lucy Honeychurch regains her vision in Italy because Italy offers her "the most priceless of all possession her own sou!."[27] She learnt the meaning of love:

> "She has learnt you will let me talk freely, as I have begun freely she has learnt what it is to love: the greatest lesson, some people will tell you, that our earthy life provides."[28]

Mr. Emerson believes in the sanity of passion and the tenderness of love. He succeeds in bringing Lucy and George Emerson together. While they are basking in the reliant sunshine of love and joy, Mr. Beebe the advocate of celibacy suddenly assumes the looks of a friend:

> "He is very quit, and his white face, with its ruddy whiskers, seemed suddenly inhuman. A long blank column, he stood and awaited her I reply."[29]

No wonder, the theme of Forster's novels reminds us of the medieval morality plays. The forces of good and evil are engaged in desperate struggle for the possession of the soul of Lucy.

'The Longest Journey' is based on the theme of sterility and fertility. Stephen Won ham reminds us of Gino, for he is the instinctual man. In 'A Room With a View', Forster trusts body and relies on love which is the function of the body. In 'The Longest Journey', Forster trusts the earth and relies on the natural man who identifies himself with nature, its the theme of search for identify. Sir James Fraser in the Golden Bough,' explains the descent of perse phone into the lower world as mythical expression of the sowing of the seed and her reappearance in spring as signifying the sprouting of the young com; "the parsephone of one year becomes the Diameter of the next."[30]

In 'The Longest Journey' Stephen Wonham loves the earth. Mrs. Failing, like Rickie's father, has "the same affliction the same heartlessness." Rickie does not get love from her:

> "He would not have asked much: as for 'Prospects', they never entered his head; but she was his only near relative, and a little kindness and hospitality during the lovely years would have made incalculable differences."[31]

The content in the novel is between conventions and nature. Stephan Wonham is in conventional, instinctual and brutal. He has in his room only one picture.

Diameter is the Goddess of Fecundity and she saves Stephen Wonham from sterility. Rickie Eliot is in the grip of conventions which create illusion:

> "He thought of Renen, who declares that on the Acropolis at Athens beauty and wisdom do exist, really exist, as external powers. He did not aspire to beauty or wisdom, but he prayed to be delivered from the shadow of unreality that had begun to darken the world."[32]

Rickie is unable to distinguish falsehood from truth, appearance from reality. In his eyes, Gerald is a god and Agnes a goddess. There are many degrees of falsehood and many levels of truth and only a man with a clear vision can see through the various disguises which falsehood usually puts on to deceive him. Ansell and Stephen Wonham are able to know truth. Ansell with his clear intellect Stephan Wonham with his intuition, and the two together are able to destroy unreality. Robert the young farmer who ran away with Mrs. Elliot, knows the vitality of the soil the passion of youth. Robert is the child of the aged soil of Wiltshire:

> "As he talked, the earth became a living being or rather being with a living skin, and manner no longer dirty stuff, but a symbol of regeneration and the birth of life from life."[33]

The social types are protected by conventions whereas the natural man is protected by the earth. Mr. Pembroke believes in firmness, discipline, good form, and team work:

> "Organize', systematize; fill up every moment; induce esprit de corps."[34]

Stephen Wonham, the unconventional man, understand Wiltshire the soil of Wiltshire as a real, living, and vigorous force. The theme of 'The Longest Journey' is based on man's salvation through the soil.

'Only connect' is the motto of 'Howards End' deals with the theme of the outer life and the inner life. It also describes them theme of a voyage for spirituality. Happiness as possible for the individual in this world provided he has adequate imagination and sufficient insight and an access to the inner life. There is, therefore a need of connection between the outer life of action and the inner life of private affections. The gulf between the two aspect of life is quite wide and can be reduced, if not actually bridged, by means of personal relationships and through the agency of nature. The outer life of practical middle-class lays stress upon property, propriety, family, pride, and conventional morality. The outer life of action, however, is meaningless for it invariably ends in panicad emptiness.

The inner life, on the other hand, is ending for it is based on the idea of the good and the beautiful. It pays in the coin of love and tenderness. The Wilcoxes in 'Howards End' are the embodiment of the solid qualities of the English middle-class. They have energy, grit, and determination. Their hands are on "all the ropes". They touched the great outer life which breeds character not sloppiness.

They are practical intelligent efficient, and successful, but quit useless to "God or Man". The whole Wilcox family is a "Fraud". They have starved the life of the sprit. Their life is excitable but without tenderness, hurried but without any sense of direction, restless but without commitment to a living faith. Henry Wilcox lacks imagination, sympathy, tenderness, poetry and passion. His life within has "reverted to chaos." Henry Wilcox does not knowhow to love and he cannot understand Margaret.

If Henry had shown real affection, she would have understood, for effecting explains everythings seemed without sentiment.[35]

The aim of Margaret is to reconcile the unseen life with the seen. Margaret writes to Helen. Don't broad too much, she wrote to Helen, on the superiority of the unseen to the seen. It's true, but to brood on it is medieval. Our business is not to contrast the two, but to reconcile them, It is Margaret who realises the need of harmony which can be achieved through the philosophy of "Only Connect," she wants to marry Henry Wilcox because she thinks that also would be able to connect sense and sensibility:

> Margaret greeted her lord with peculiar tenderness. Mature as he was, she might yet be able to help him to the building of the rainbow bridge that should connect the prose in us with the passion, without it we are Meaningless, Fragments, half Monks, half beasts, unconnected arches that have never. Joined into a Man.[36]

Margaret fails to connect the feminine sprit with the masculine sprit. In the end, however, she is aware of a unity through 'Hawards End' and the 'Wychdm' through the house that connects man with his ancestors and with the generations to come, and through the tree that symbolizes strength, tenderness and permanence.

It was neither warrior, nor lover, nor god, in none of these roles do the English excel. It was a comrade, bending over the house strength and adventure in its roots, but in that a dozen men could not have spanned, become in the end evanescent, till pale bud clusters seemed to float in the air.[37]

Illusions and their die leaving behind silence and emptiness. Reality, have has three important aspects which are made concrete in the three parts of the Novel—"Mosque", "Caves" and "Temple", the subject of the novel has been stated by Foreter thus.

He long in a trance, sensuous but healthy, through which the talks of the two others did not seem particularly sad they were discussing as to whether it is possible to be friends with an Englishman Mahmood Ali argued that it was not. Hamidullah disagreed, but with so many reservation that was no fractions between them.[38]

Dr. Arnold kettle comments that "it is typical of Forster to make no bones about stating his theme".

Forster's vision has conceived and developed the theme. His pagan outlook is revealed in his bringing out the contact between the two modes of life. The conventional and the natural in 'Where Angles Fear to Tread'. His anti-medieval outlook seem in 'A Room With a View' whole he glorifies but condemns the medieval concept of asceticism. 'The Longest Journey' deals with the various disguises which falsehood puts an end there by and causes confusion in the mind. Forster's individualistic approach to life is evident in Howards End. Where he wants to connect the outer life with the inner life. And finally his prophetic vision is evident in A Passage to India. The social theme takes the form of satire and the comedy of manner, the natural theme the forms of fantasy while the theme of appearances and reality, takes the form of Prophecy.

References

1. Leavis, F. R., *The Common Persuit.* A peregrine book -1962
2. Forster, E.M.: *Howords End* (London, Edward Arnold 1910) p. 82.
3. Forster. E. M., *A Passage to India* (London Edward Arnold 1924) p. 192.
4. *Ibid.,* p. 193.
5. *Ibid.,* p. 201.
6. *Ibid.,* p. 222.
7. *Ibid.,* p. 284.
8. Choudhary, Nirad C., *A Passage to End From India.* (New Delhi).
9. Jones, E. B. C., E. M. Foster and Virginia Woolf; *The Enqlish Novelists* (London 1936), p. 272.
10. Hoare, Dorothy M., *Some Studies in the Modem Novel* (Philadelphia 1953), p. 80.
11. Woolf, Virginia, The Novels of E.M. Forster," *The Death of the Moth and Other Essays* (London 1942), p. 105.
12. Forster E.M., *Two Cheers for Democracy* —"The Challenge of Our Time."
13. *Ibid.,* p. 67.
14. Arnold Matthew, "Dover Beach", *Poetry and Prose* (London 1954) p. 145.
15. Oliver H.J.: *The Art of E.M. Forster* (Melbourne Univ. Press 1960), p. 13.
16. Cecil, David: *Poets and Story Tellers* (London 1949), p. 183.
17. Forster, E.M., *Two Cheers for Democracy.* "What I believe", p. 77.
18. Forster E.M., *Howards End* (London Edward Arnold 1910), p. 77.
19. Tindall, W. Y., *Forces in Modern British Literature* (New York 1949), p. 365.

20. Forster, E.M., *Where Angles Fear to Tread* (London Edward Arnold 1905) p. 94.
21. *Ibid.*, pp. 153-54.
22. *Ibid.*, p. 150.
23. Holt, Elbert Lee: *E.M. Forster and Samuel Butler*, P.M.L.A. Vol. LXI, p. 805.
24. Forster E.M., *A Room With a View* (London Edward Arnold 1907), p. 93.
25. *Ibid.*, p. 18.
26. *Ibid.*, p. 32.
27. *Ibid.*, p. 118.
28. *Ibid.*, p. 108.
29. *Ibid.*, p. 217.
30. Frazer, James: *The Golden Bough*, 1922 (London 1954), p. 422.
31. Forster E.M., *The Longest Journey* (London Edward Arnold. 1908), p. 115.
32. *Ibid.*, p. 173.
33. *Ibid.*, p. 258.
34. *Ibid.*, p. 299.
35. Forster E.M., *Howards End* (London Edward Arnold 1910), p. 194.
36. *Ibid.*, p. 174.
37. *Ibid.*, p. 192.
38. Kettle, Arnold, E.M. Forster *A Passage to India, An Introduction to the English Novel*, Vol. II (London 1953), p. 153.

3

Social Problems in Forster Novels: Treatment of English Middle-Class

As a novelist Forster belongs of his novels is the conventional English middle-class of the Edwardian era. In his novels he is mainly concerned with the moral dilemmas and personal perplexities of the sensitive men and women during that period. His novels convey his unified vision of the society and the individual. It is a double vision based on the exposure of society and the exploration of the inner life of the individual.

Society and the individual stands for contrary principles of life. Society stands for the principles of controls, the individual), on the other hand, stands for the freedom. Society prior to the Industrial Revolution, was Organic. It become impersonal when the social being was torn as under from the true self, and business relationships took the place of personal relationships. Social being in the Modern bourgeois society are hold together by class consciousness. Possessive instinct, self-interest, and money value. "Cash is the music of labour in bourgeois society."[1] The middle-class is conventional. The bourgeois sprit shows its" Preoccupation with outer life, with the things of the body, and its obliviousness to the needs of the soul.[2] If suffers from stresses and strains of social relationships. Disintegration in urban civilization is a "Menace to every form of life".

"Society no longer offers the appearance of an entity, but is mislead conceived as an aggregate of conflicting forces."[3]

The problems of the novel has always been to distinguish the two kinds of reality, the social reality and the individual self. The individual can't ignore society since he can live the life of a recluse. The novelist, too, can't ignore society and he has to take notice of it.

"And in every case society is there, to be taken account of and accepted as a basic fact about human life even when the author wishes to attack it."[4]

The individual, in the interest of the creative work, must not be swallowed up by society, 'literature', according to Sir Maurice Bowra, 'By recognizing the worth of the individual emphasizes the importance of the liner life and, in doing so reflects something absolutely vital to the world.[5] The social stuff is transferred when it comes into contact with the true self of wan. The individual is a live center of spirituality, his body and his word are, "but hollow husks of the inner self, which is the only reality."[6]

The recovery of the self, is the triumph of art, for the artist has snatched a trophy which belongs to the domain of philosophy. The novel is the study of man in society, and its vision is 'social'. The novel is also the study of man centered in the true self, and its vision is "Private".

Society and self according to Mark Schorer are "perhaps the basic terms of the work, whereas appearance and reality are the basic terms of all art".[7] The novel seems to exist at a point of intersection of society and self:

> "The novel seems to exist at a point where we can recognize the intersection of the stream of social history and the stream of soul."[8]

The poles of novelistic tension are society and self, appearance and reality. Carvantes brought society and self-together is a durable antithesis by dealing with 'the shakes and toads' of the social facts and 'the vision entertained by the self, Sancho Panza falls "Into a very deep hole."

"Here we are like to perish with deadly hunger, I and my ass. If we don't die before, he of his bruises and I of Grief and Anguish: at least I shan't be so lucky as was my master Don Quixote, when he went down into the cave of the Enchanter Montesines. He found better fare there than he could have at his own house, the cloth was laid, and his Bed made, and he saw nothing but pleasant visions: But I am like to see nothing here but toads and shakes."[9]

Fiction exists not merely to criticize and protest but also to immortalize what it creates. Forster, in his novels, brings together society and self in juxtaposition so as to bring out the contrast between the false and the true. His outer vision exposes the evils of society: his inner vision, on the other hand, reveals the glories of self. Funding bourgeois society crippled by conventions. Forster seeks an escape from the horror of social life. In an artist. "The Ivory Tower" Published in London mercury, December, 1938 Forster wrote about the the hard, the community, and the world and his desire to escape from the external world into the private life.[10] Forster finds joy in the inner life. He is interested in self, true and significant. Dr. Leavis's.

> "But for Blake the conventional order had no interest, and conventional expression falsified or ignored what individual experience told him was the real, the true and the significant".[11]

Forster is pessimistic about society because it promises order but never succeeds in achieving it, he has, however, a mystic faith in the individual:

> "He seems to me a devise achievement and I mistrust any view which belittles him."[12]

The novelist has to avoid both the harshness of the 'rigorous view,' and the laxity of the, 'permissive view'. He has to get as close as he can to two aspects of life human nature and morality. Sexual morality and religion relate directly "to the basic constituents of human nature: the libidinal impulses, and aggression".[13] Through morality, society tries to control the primitive instincts: through religion, the aggressive instincts. The most important single theme in organized faith is, "the teaching about death and personal survival." In the novels of Forster there is neither the 'rigorous view 'nor the laxity of the Permissive view.' His novels are a plea to life of the English middle-class in Edwardian England.

Forster's novels are written on the plan of two levels the realistic and the imaginative. The classic intuition of the novelist is the investigation of social reality, while the romantic intuition of the novelist is the exploration of the understanding of the triviality of social reality and also on the awareness of the private life.

"The novel then, is a perpetual quest for reality," the field of its research being always the social world, the material of its analysis being always manners as the indication of the directions of main's soul."[14]

Forster's novels expresses the triumph of the human spirit over falsehood, of the victory of the soul over the evils of society. Infect his novels have been interpreted as "a defense of the heart against the potential arrogance of the mind."[15] Forster by taking up the subject of the social thought, deals with the interaction of the two types of character, the intersection of two planes of living in his novels. The conflict between those who live by convention and those who live by instinct. The world of convention is described by Forster with "keen observation and keen satire."[16] while the world of instinct and emotion is described with poetic gusto.

Forster in a television interview has stated that the social aspect of the world has changed so much that he cannot put the new world into fiction:

> "I had been accustomed to write about the old fashioned world with its home and its family life and its comparative peace, all that went, and though I can think about the new world I cant put it into fiction."

The starting point of the short stories and the novels of Forster is the social being who is leading a secure life within the framework of society. The core of society is convention. The things that matter in bourgeois society are birth, respectability, wealth and pseudo-culture. The gravest dangers to society are instincts, passions, yearnings and dreams. The life of the social being is ordered. The individual on the other hand, is free and he draws his strength from his inner convictions, his sense of beauty, and his healthy instincts. In the novels of Forster, society is opposed to self: "the good, the beautiful, the true is opposed to the respectable the pretty, the adequate".[17] Progress, expansion/efficiency and self-interest are the characteristic of the industrial civilization. The social being deprived of his humanity becomes assertive. In a conventional society world, as revealed by Forster in fictional form, is "a Cheerless, loveless world.[18] Forster in his short stories has attacked the English middle-class for its practical outlook and purblind morality. Edwin Honig calls Forster "we discover a criticism of civilized society's inability to produce an integrated individualism."[19] Forster believes that through the pastoral way of life men, in an artificial atmosphere of civilized society, can "regain the world of beauty, goodness, truth, of friendship, love, and magnanimity—those lost images of free community among men."[20]

The short stories of Forster are a vigorous protest against "material progress and urban convention."[21] Forster in his novels has criticized the English middle-class for its bourgeois spirit its money making mentality, its insistence on material prosperity, its lack of culture, its social-killing vulgarity, its deadness of beauty, its customary morality, and its smug complacency, Forster through Greek mythology, denounces the cross materialism of the bourgeoisic. He has faith in the instinctive life which is infallible; and he has faith in the natural, the spontaneous, and the human way of life. Forster, it seems is still learning the craft of fiction, form and theme have not been blended in a coherent whole in his novels.

However, he explores the basic theme and other themes in his minor fiction.

Sawston, in "where Angels Fear to tread" is convention–ridden and stands for respectability, morality, purity dullness, mediocrity and all the cardinal virtues of the English middle-class. Philip Harriton is full of passion for Italy and ridicules the sacred institutions of Sawston "the book club, the debating society, the progressive whist, the bazaars."[22] Thereby shocking Harriet Harriton who is a strong willed and ill tempered fanatic. It is Miss Abbott good, quiet, dull, and amiable who rebels against Sawston and its way.

"All that winter I seemed to be waking up to beauty and splendor and I don't know what: and when the spring come, I wanted to fight against the things I hated-mediocrity and dullness and spitefulness and society."[23]

Mrs. Harriton is diplomatic and insensible: "Her life, he saw, was without wearing. To what purpose was her diplomacy, her, insincerity, and her continued repression of vigour? Did they even bring happiness or her self?"[24] Mrs. Harriton is a 'Useless machine'.

"Harriet with her gloomy pervish creed, Lilia with her clutches after than this well ordered, active, useless machine."[25]

Miss Abbott hates Sawston and its conventions but she becomes aware of the power of conventions over the individual. Philip Harriton, on the other hand, is aware of the invincibility of the true self. The individual can escape from the dullness and mediocrity of conventional life into the splendor and beauty of the inner life:

> "Society is invincible to a certain degree. But your real life is your own, and nothing can touch it. There is no power on earth that can prevent your criticizing and despising mediocrity-nothing that can stop you retreating into splendor and beauty–into the thoughts and beliefs that make that real life–the real you."[26]

The Swastonians stands for the life on negation they never learn to be sincere, they never learn how to enjoy themselves and they spend their lives in making little sacrifices for objects they don't care for. The conventional people, according to Forster, are not enlightened. They are false and benighted. Lucy honey church, in 'A Room with a view,' joins the vast armies of the benighted':

> "She gave up trying to understand herself and joined the vast armies of the benighted, who follow neither the heart nor the brain and march to their destiny by catch-words."[27]

Forster attacks falsehood: "The armour of falsehood is subtly wrought out of darkness, and hides a man not only from others, but from his own soul."[28]

Society, thus, stands for convention, falsehood and unreality, whereas the individual stands for reality, truth and goodness. The Conflict in the novels of forester, is between society and self. " Between the real and the pretended."[29]

In "Where Angels Fear to Tread" we find conversion through transformation of the character and fulfillment through positive joy. Philip is saved in the end because he discovers his true self. "Where Angle Fear to Tread" according to Dr. Leavis is "the most-successful of the pre-war novels."[30]

"A Room With a View" is truly written in the Meredithian spirit of romantic comedy. Its theme is the eternal social theme of comedy, namely the clash between illusion and reality. Lucy Honeychurch wants to live in a world, which is free, natural, joyful, and life giving. But she is stifled in the stuffy atmosphere of propriety. The obstacles to the freedom of the individual in society are many social barriers customary morality and petty conventions prevent the individual from enjoying a free and full life. The theme of 'A room with a view' is the theme of self-discovery and self-realization. It is based on a war against intellectual and emotional narrowness of English middle-class. It is a plea for the natural life which is uninhibited and care free.

'A Room With a View' has a mythology of its own. The vital forces of life fight against muddle and convention. Its glance is mischievous and it exposes self-consciousness and pretended virtue.

The social aspect is at war with the bourgeois spirit which itself off from the true being. Sawston in the novels of Forster represses the forces of vitality and is protected from the wild raiders of beauty, joy and love. Forster, the satirist, ridicules the idleness and the dullness of the social types through Miss Abbott and Gino. Mrs. Harriton is described as a social machine, cold, inhuman, ruthless and quite useless. Forster has nothing but contempt for Mrs. Harriton who is diplomatic, insincere and hypocritical. She wears a mask of respectability and propriety but underneath the pleasant exterior she hides a nature, which is mean, selfish, and spiteful. Forster criticizes the conventional characters like Mrs. Harriton and Harriet, who care for principles and not for the welfare of the baby of Gino:

> "It was to be low church, it was to be high-principled, it was to be tactful gentlemanly, artistic-excellent things all."[31]

Cecil Vyse, in 'A Room With a View' is satirized by Forster for he is conceited priggish, pampous and pretentious. Cecil Vyse is an egoist and Lucy breaks off her engagement and has wrapped himself in art and books and music, where she wants to live a life of freedom.

'The satirist', says Prof. James Southerland in "English satire", is critical of society and is at war with the pretensions of society.' The interpretation of society is a disadvantage to the writer when it imposes a limitation on his art. The satirist seems not the human being but a particular folly. He gains in simplicity and clarity but loses in richness, subtlety, and depth. The true satirist possesses a double vision for he exposes society and explores self. His vision is not only negative but also positive. He civilizes the society, but out of criticisms he is able to create a vision of the good life. A satirist possesses mind which is quick and not "slow and cumbersome."[32] Infect "the quickness, the delicacy of touch and the precision."[33] Go to make satire, Forster's double attitude to life make him the great satirist of English middle-class. He possesses a quick mind, which perceives the vices and follies of the conventional people. His satire is effective and tolerant because there is always in his social comedy a burning core. What matter in his novels—is the living center:

"It is the soul; It is the reality, it is truth."[34]

Forster's social interpretation is sparklingly gay but it has a dignity, which is compounded of natural poise and an unconscious cultivation of self. His criticism of society reveals a mind, which loves the true and the natural. Behind the social satire of foster there is a vision of good life and from his vision ultimately comes a direct revelation of reality, foster is sympathetic and tolerant towards the individuals.

Forster in 'Where Angels Fear to Tread' and 'A Room With a View' lays stress on the physical aspect of shut up in the cocoon of class-consciousness and self-consciousness. In Italy, are ennobled, purged of their ego, cured of their blindness, and they are brought back to humanity.

The belief of individual salvation is important in the novels of Forster, In "Howards End" Helen says at last that the 'harvest of the hay from the field was much bigger than that year, than it had ever before, the whole background is green and it will nourish the lives of all the persons of the family. It suggests that the future of all the members of Howards End and England is how safe from any mental or physical crisis.

It Italy Lucy Honeychurch forgets the conventions of the English middle-class and she develops the real life she values tenderness, believes in personal relation ships, and discovers that love is the real source of strength. Lucy looks lovely, radiant, and joyful, and George Emerson kissed her:

> "He saw radiant joy in her face, he saw the flowers beat against her dress in blue waves. The bushes above them closed. He stepped quickly forward and kissed her."[35]

Forster, infect in his social novels uses "domestic comedy as a means of exploring social and psychological conflicts of a much more problematic kind than those of Jane Austen treats in her novels."[36]

References

1. Candwell, Christopher, Further Studies in a Dying Culture (London 1949), p. 107.
2. Savage, D.S. : The Personal Principle (London-1944), p. 25.
3. Mendilow, A. A., Time and the Novel (London-1952), p. 6.
4. Daiches, David: Critical Approaches to Literature (London-1956), p. 371.
5. Bowra, Maurice, The Study of Literature (convocation address, Birkbeck college, London, 1952), p. 12.
6. Olsen, Robert G, Authenticity Metaphysics and Moral Responsibility (Philosophy vol. 34, 1959), p. 104.
7. Schorer, Mark: Society and Self in the Novel (Newyork -1956), pp. 14-15.
8. *Ibid.*, p. 11.
9. Cervantes, Mignel de . Don Quixote (modern library-Newyork 1950) p. 812.
10. Forster, E.M., Quoted by A. C. Ward in 20th Century Literature, 1928 (London Vol. 12, 1956), p. 17.
11. Leavis, F. R., Revaluation (London-1953), p. 124.
12. Forster, E.M., Two Cheers for Democracy, 'The Challenge of our Time', p. 68.
13. Wollheim, Richard: Deception and shook (Encounter, Vol. 18 Jan., 1962), p. 15.
14. Trilling, Lionall, Manners, Moral and the Novels, "The Liberal Imagination (London-1951), p. 212.
15. Toynbee Philip, Novel Through Forster's Glass (*The Hindustan Times, Sunday magazine,* Jan. 4, 1950), p. 4.
16. Encyclopaedia Britannica, Vol. ix (Chicago-1949), p. 520.
17. Forster, E.M., Howards End (London, Edward Arnold 1910), p. 160.

18. Forster, E.M., A Room With A View (London Edward Arnold) p. 86.

19. Honig, Edwin: Dark Conceit (London-1959) p. 166.

20. *Ibid.*, p. 169.

21. Grandson K.W. : E.M. Forster (London 1962) p. 166.

22. Forster E.M. : Where Angels Fear To Tread (London Edward Arnold 1905) p. 14.

23. *Ibid.*, p. 69.

24. *Ibid.*, p. 77.

25. *Ibid.*, pp. 77-78.

26. *Ibid.*, p. 69.

27. Forster E.M., A Room With A View (London- Edward Arnold 1908), p. 18.

28. *Ibid.*, p. 172.

29. *Ibid.*, p. 172.

30. Leavis F.R., " E.M. Forster" The Common Pursuit, 1952 (A Peregrine Book, 1962), p. 262.

31. Forster, E.M., Where Angels Fear To Tread (London Edward Arnold 1905), p. 113.

32. Woolf, Virginia: George Eliot "The Common Reader 1925" (London 1948), p. 212.

33. Leavis, F.R., "George Eliot", The Great Tradition (London 1948) p. 8.

34. Woolf, Virginia, "The Novels of E.M. Forster." The Death of The Moth and Other Stories (London), p. 48.

35. Other Essays, 1942 (London 1947) p. 105.

36. Forster E.M., A Room With A View (London Edward Arnold 1908), p. 75.

4

E.M. Forster: As a Humanist

"I belong to the fag-end of Victorian liberalism".

E.M. Forster in a
B.B.C. broadcast in 1946

The age of Forster is also known as the age of great 'liberal tradition'. The term liberal have many connotations. It may imply an open hearted free thinker as well as a person who compromises between change and tradition. In the context of the late 19th century Victorian thought, liberalism broadly indicates belief in democracy, freedom, extension of franchise, social reform, economic justice, abolition of slavery, free trade and other related ideas of the middle-class ethos. Its basic source was conscience. The Victoreans were earnest about the promptings of their conscience and consequently formulated their attitudes which make the liberal tradition. Liberalism in early 20th century before the World War was an extension of this great Victorean heritage of the Gladstone and Bentham, Mill and Morley, though in its process of growth it had undergone several changes.

Forster belongs to "the fag end of Victorian liberalism".[1] It was the great middle-class liberalism which, in the mid-Victorian period, supported freedom of enterprise and free trade, advocated local self-government, practiced benevolence, uphold free speech, introduced social reforms, and "entertained a sincere faith in the progress of society". Liberalism, had its roots in Utilitarianism. Self-help, earnest endeavour, thrift and duty were the typical mid-Victorian virtues. 'Laissez-faire' came to be regarded by the English middle-class as the key to success, prosperity, comfort, and security. Freedom of thought was the essence of Liberalism. Forster aligned himself with those liberals who "rejected laissez faire economics while preserving and reinterpreting the liberal ideal of individualism".[2] Individual freedom, tolerance, and power of reason constitute, in fact, the "outlook of the free spirit" Forster has faith in individual freedom, parliamentary institutions, racial equality, good-will and toleration. The real threat to the free spirit, according to Forster, is due to political encroachment on individual freedom and also due to social interference. The individualist believes in the worth and dignity of man; he believes in "liberty and variety and tolerance and sympathy."[3] The humanist considers this world real, emphasizes the dignity of man and the worth of human life, tends to place reason above revelation, and stresses self-education and self-development. Humanism, in fact "makes for breadth, tolerance equilibrium and sanity."[4] The novelist, as a humanist, shows "curiosity a free mind, belief in good taste belief in the human race."[5] Forster is an individualist and he always lays stress on the humanistic values that really do matter tolerance good temper and sympathy; the natural warmth of personal relationships; the worth of individual and the love for all types of men. His stress is on love which eternally triumphant.[6] Forster believes that an aristocracy of the sensitive, the considerate and the plucky alone, can restore the moral balance which has been disturbed as a result of the scientific advancement and the technological progress in modern times. It goes to the credit of Forster that he is an individualist in an age which believes in regimentation and efficiency. Forster's literary life started when the first number of the Independent Review appeared in October 1903. He contributed short stories and "cultural essays" to it.

The liberalism of Forster reminds us of J.S. Mill's concept of private liberty—the freedom of the individual from the tyranny of society the curtailment of social checks and restraints upon the individual, the development of personality the recognition of individual differences and variety, the importance of felling in human life and the worth of the private life. Forster calls himself a bourgeois: he "adheres to the British constitution."[7]; he believes in "the preservation and the extension of freedom"; he wants to keep open a few breathing holes for the human spirit[8]; and he loves the countryside which is still left untouched by the ugliness and the sameness of the urban civilization.[9] Forster's Lawgivers are Erasmus and Montaigne, not Moses and St. Paul. Like Erasmus, Forster is opposed to orthodoxy, religious fanaticism, intolerance and violence.

Like Montaigne, Forster is an upholder of the humanistic values and an implacable enemy of cocksureness. The agnostic mind of Forster shows that he is the child of unbelief. His motto is : "Lord, I disbelieve, help thou my unbelief." Christianity, according to Forster, was "a spiritual force once";[10] and the "indwelling spirit" will have to be probably Restated "in a non-Christian form", if it is to retain its influence in modern society. Forster deplores Christianity's hatred of carnality, and he criticizes its intolerance of heresy and its contempt for secular truth. Forster's electicism, however, has been misunderstood by devout Christians as scepticism. Forster in Aspects of the Novel writes:

> "The human mind is not a dignified organ, and I do not how we can exercise it sincerely except through electicism".[11]

The sceptical humanist in E.M. Forster is plainly present in Abinger Harvest: "Our life on earth is, and ought to be, material and carnal.[12]" Life may also be more chance, but she has evolved the imposing doctrine of effort and reward to obscure her purposelessness.[13] Liberalism, according to Lionel Trilling, "drifts towards a denial of the emotions and the imagination"; when looked at in a critical spirit, there is noticed in Liberalism a discrepancy between "the primal imagination of liberalism and its present particular manifestations"; and the recognition of this discrepancy between theory and practice implies "the awareness of complexity and difficulty."[14] Forster, the novelist, is aware of the "ironies and disappointments inherent in humanism". In theory, Forster remains loyal to the ideal of liberal humanism, but as a novelist he "finds himself drawn more and more to its negative side."[15] Dr. Arnold Kettle has rightly pointed out that in the discussion of Forster's liberalism "the parties of it all use the word liberalism with variations of meaning."

"It is a dangerous game to try to pin E.M. Forster down. And yet such words as liberal, individualist, agonistic, certainly help, though I think they refer more usefully to his attitudes than to a more specific, coherent philosophy."[16] Forster is as usual modest about his role as a liberal, but one should not assume that he is belittling liberalism or his role in its modern development. In fact Forster involvement in the liberal tradition was mutually enriching to both the parties. On the one hand, Forster stood to gain from the liberal perspective, he adopted towards life around him. On the other hand, the liberal tradition received new life and impetus from its most creative involvement is best expressed. In his novels where, urban and scrupulous, tentative yet traditional, the liberal Forster confronts us with a series of searching, even sceptical, questions about the purposes of life and civilization.

In all his novels, Forster states his commitment to that loose body of middle-class opinion known as 'Liberalism' which says that it is up to every man to choose his own friend, his own job, to arrive at his own convictions etc. Forster is an advocate of reason, intelligence, culture, tolerance and civilization against barbarity and provincialism. Accompanying these qualities is a fervent belief in individual freedom, as intense enthusiasm for the art and a passionate hatred of all forms of the authoritarianism, including imperialism. In keeping with this liberal humanitarian outlook, Forster speaks out against the manners and morals of the British middle-class. He satrizes its callous soldiers and smug officials, redicules its business ethics, and more generally, its class-consciousness. The pragmatist that he is, Forster is aware that the ruling class has been able to provide trade, commerce and a civilized social system to the community. But in the process, Forster the liberal humanist, notes that there have been a weakening of human sympathy and understanding. The British educational system is to blame of this, since it neglects the emotions and, by overvaluing restraint as a means of developing character, it impairs sensitively. In his book 'Two cheers for Democracy' he deplore the middle-class public-school ideal and its consequences, which he sees as the stunting of personality and the instillation of prejudice. The product of this system. He writes, "go forth into a world that is not entirely composed of public school men or even of Anglo-Saxons, but of men who are as various the sands of the sea; into a world of whose richness and suletty they have no conception. They go forth into it with well developed bodies, fairly developed minds, and undeveloped hearts. And it is this undeveloped heart that is largely responsible for the difficulties of Englishman abroad."[17]

Although a rationalist Forster, like Lawrence and Verginia Woolf, was convinced that life was something more than merely mental. A love of the bright pagon life of the senses, of impulse and spontaneous emotions, drew him to the Greeks, but his fastidious intelligence and innate dualism forced him to distrust the imaginative vision of life even while he succumbed to its inspirations. He was far from the accepting Lawrence's religion of the blood and would have shrunk from a conception of human personality that was based on repulsion and that the 'wisdom of the heart' had been to little considered in the 19th century, with the result that in spite of material progress, there had been a weakening of human sympathy and understanding. Englishman were especially to be blamed in this, the emotions and by over-valuing restraint as a means of developing character, they inspaired sensitivity, hence he attacks on the public-schools.

Forster perceived the peculiar dilemma confronting liberalism in the 20th century. Liberalism was based on reason it had rejected theology; its chief exponents were agnostic or vaguely pantheist. Moreover, reason which had denied the force of imagination was itself in danger of being swept away by irrational impulses the more presence of which indicates an unadmitted hunger of the human soul for deeper satisfaction that trade, commerce and civilized social system could provide. Reason was obviously not enough but the alternatives were alarming and uncontrollable. Forster's problem was how to reconcile civilized order with imaginative awareness and the world of feeling.

E.M. Forster's values were those of 'Bloomsbury Group' of writers, artists and intellectuals. They were called the 'Bloomsburg' group because many of them at time or another had flats in the agreeable district of London, called 'Bloomsburg'. This group flourished soon after the death of the Queen Victoria until the II World War. They were all the followers of the Cambridge philosopher G.E. Moore, the author of 'Principia Ethika' who taught them the importance of good and pleasant states of feeling in the individual human life. In all of them, therefore, there is a kind of passionate striving towards charity, goodwill and understanding and towards a perception of the passing but real beauty of the world. The good is to be found in individual experience and, though men and women are mortal, the good as not less real.

This refined and difficult but by no means sentimental philosophy is also known as liberal tradition. Speaking about this group G.H. Thompson says:

> "There is not exactly a lack of warmth in their writing, but there is sometimes a rather frightening assumption that the most of the human 'living is mere muddle and waste, and that only a few successful lives, those of intellectuals and artist, are truly civilized people; in short really count through of course at the same time the lives of 'outsiders' may, of the civilized

people, have a value of pathos or comedy. At the same time, most of these writers, perhaps all of them, were humanitarianism did not spring, however, any self-identification with the struggling and suffering masses of the people, but rather from an impatience with what seemed to them irrational and untidy and destructive in ordinary life. Their pity was real but a little cold."[18]

Though Forster belongs to this early Edwardian liberal tradition, but his responses to it are mixed. He is in tune with the liberal tradition and he is also out of step with it. In areas such as belief in democracy and individual freedom, he is a great votary of liberalism, but he is impatient with its economic policies and unrestricted concentration of wealth in the hands of the few to the disadvantage of the many. Forster realizes the full implication of Disraeli's description of Victorian England on consisting of two nations, the have's and the have nots, and the need to bridge. The gap from excessive wealth to extreme poverty. He has been an agonizing witness to the gradual decay of liberalism after the World War I. As an individualist he saw "liberalism crumbling beneath him and at first felt ashamed," but soon realized that 'there was no special reason for shame. Forster is almost prophetic in realizing the impending decay of liberalism in England and therefore he shows a new awareness of another, more progressive, scale of values. He desires a synthesis between what he calls the old morality, based on socialistic principles. It is interesting to note that Forster's notions have in fact been translated into action in present day Britain.

Order culture, tolerance, admirable as they were in themselves, were so often balanced by hardness, complacency and insensitivity and by the absence of the vital principle that give richness and joy to life. Those who were the pillars of society, respected guardians of the civilizations, often lacked heart and were devoid of tenderness. Down in the ripe human jungle among the swamps of passion, both good and evil pulsated with stronger and more intense life than on the cleared cultivated uplands. According to Forster, who considered this problem in relation to England, the English man's weakness lay in his 'undeveloped heart', which prevented him from understanding the richness and subtlety in the world about him. This world's confused complexity of human characters and relationship is the chief theme of Forster's novel.

A peculiar inconclusiveness underlies much of Forster's philosophy and may have its origin in liberal tradition to which he belongs. Although he champions the good life and delights in beauty, nature and the warm impulses of man, Forster has no massage for the spirit. Like Verginia Woolf, and for similar reason, he is aware of the confusion and mystery that lie at the heart of life and, like her, believes that it is beyond men's efforts to understand. Belonging to a generation that denied the existence of the absolute values, rejected the theological dogmas of the middle ages and was unable to anticipate a regenerated Christianity, Forster found that their was nothing go left but to contemplate the mystery and to hope that some how civilizations would gradually weaken it and cause it to disappear. To the end, Forster remained a follower of intellectual 'Laissez Faire', putting his trust, but not to confidently, in that civilized solvent of hatred and prejudices sweet reasonableness and toleration.

This central concept of Bloomsbury philosophy is closely linked with belief in efficacy of personal relations he says in 'Howards End':

> "Personal relations are the important thing for ever and ever and not then other life of telegram and anger".

Faith in personal relationship is central to Forster's credo yet he is not blind to the limitations placed on them officially.[19]

Forster says in 1939 in his essay 'What I Believe' : "I had his ideas of caused and if I had to choose between betraying my country and betraying my friends, I hope I should the guts to betray by country",[20] personal relation are a fundamentally good value for Forster and from them follows his passion for truth, tolerance, good temper and sympathy in personal relations. According to him, civilization constitutes that period in history when force and violence have not prevailed over tolerance and sympathy a period in which all the great creative actions and all the decent human relations tend to occur.

In keeping with these convictions Forster's novel have, as their subject matter, the breaking down of barriers between white and black, between class and class, between man and woman between art and life. Only connect is the motto of 'Howards End' mightbe the motto of all his work to put forward his liberal case effectively. Forster employs a unique strategy: he presents a philistine society that has been corrupted by materialism and complacency and prejudice and opposes the values of this society, by the values of the good heart. In the first three novels, we are taken to be the world of Swastone, whose people blinded by materialism and prejudice have become complacent and insensitive. They are so well entranced in their society that they have developed a blindness to the dull squalor and vulgarity of a commercial world which has degraded man into a mere getting and spending animal and has reduced society to a network of impersonal relationships. Forster eloquently satirizes a crude philistinism of such a society throughout his novels. Thus in 'Where Angels Fear to Tread' the Harriton hope to discuss Gino, the Italian husband of their daughter, by offering a thousand lira, later they are willing to pay all they have in order to obtain Gino's child, and when it can't be bought it is stolen. In "Howards End" Wilcox the business man can think of others only as trying to get something out of him. When Margaret tries to face him with his personal betrayal of his former liaison with Jaky, his moral obtuseness prevents him from feeling anything about it; he cries not only because his pocket and reputation are touched. In "A passage to India", we see how the Anglo-Indians have built a stale word of their own blind and empty to the richness of Indian civilization around them.

The liberal tradition is a tradition which says, it is up

to every men to choose his own friends, his own job, to arrive at him own convictions. And the liberal education is an education which, opposed to a mechanical education, will enlarge and humanise the mind and not merely prepares a man to earn his living at some particular trade, Forster then is a novelist not only is isolated individualism but a tradition of normal independence in the individual which has helped in the past to serve for Great Britain: social justice and peace. Hence with the novel of E.M. Forster the full tide of the liberal humanist tradition is encountered, end that Forster is a liberal and a humanist who loved civilization.

As Forster himself says that tie belong to the end of Victorian liberalism the tone of comic self-depreciation is a typical and also misleading, since it soon becomes clear that Forster is by no means throwing away the values which he grow up although he recognizes that it was not only inevitable, but right that the economic bases which had given then an appearance stability should have been undermined. This chapter will be concerned only incidentally with the politics and economics of his liberalism and will be directed two question: (1) how illuminating is it to consider Forster as coming at the end of a tradition? and (2) how far it is justifiable to explain the slightness and indeterminacy which genuine admires have found in his works in term of the fact that he came not only at the end of a tradition but at the feg end of it—at a time when its energies, if actually at their last gasp, were burning low?

Literary tradition are complex things, and merely to sketch the outline of the one, and indicate a few of its landmarks is liable to do injustice to its richness and variety. But in this case the live of development which must have had a profound influence both upon the pattern of values to be found in the novels and on the method used to deeply, it, is a very familiar one, and it is only Forster's association with it which seems to have been insufficiently acknowledged. His strategy in all five of the novels in basically a simple one, and may be summed up in the world 'confrontation'. He presents a society which has been depersonalised by materialism, philistinism, some of the more inhibiting forms of Puritanism and most of all perhaps by blinding complacency enquendered by a confidant sense of its own entrenchment. The small town or the sub urban world of the first three novels is greatly extended in the other two, and how brings in some of the makes of the wealth, and wielders of power, but the Swaston attitude survive happily enough in the metropolitan wilderness of London, and do not budge even when transplanted to Chandrapore. And the spokesman for this world whether they be Pembrokes, Herriton, Wilcoxes, Callenders, Turtons all use essentially the same language. But this language is sharply challenged in all of the novels, and here an element of complication comes in, since the Swaston voice is not by one voice, but by two. The two voice use akin that they are both on the side of 'life' – on the side that is, of a clearer richer and deeper perception of human personality and human relations than Swaston cases about or can comprehend. They therefore almost invariably combine against Swaston but at times, too, they can only salute one another from a distance or even came into regretful conflict with each other. At the risk of some simplification, the one voice may be some up in the term applied to Mrs. Wilcox 'instinctive wisdom', and the other in terms used to describe Fielding's attitude good will plus culture and intelligence. And the genuine but the uneasy relationship between them finds rather crude allegorical expression in The Longest Journey' whose Stephan, punches Ansell in the month before making friends with him, and later Ansell defends him against the Pembrokes with a sharp articulatedness which Stephen himself could not supply.

Forster invokes these two voices, and explores the virtues and limitations of each throughout the novels, and to the modern reader who would not, of course, lose the variegation provided by the social community but who recognize that with the decline in authority of the Swaston it is bound to loss some of its relevance and force it may seem that it is here that their chief interest lies. At times Forster may seen to be coming down on one side or the other, but the final effect is one of holding the balance, while delicately discriminating between the two. It is indicated, for instance in 'The Longest Journey' that the Stephan is in touch with nature; this is obviously equally true of the Emersons and Ruth Wilcox, and when we remember all those celebrations in the early stories, it may well seen that Forster upholding nature and instinct as the ideal but his attitude is surely equivocal. It is true that there is a Dionysian element more or less strong, in all the novels. 'It is their in the whole portrayal of Stephen, in the bathing scene in 'A Room with a View' in the splendid gaiety of the opera in 'where Angels fear to Tread' in the flaming ramparts of beathoven's fifth symphony in 'Howards End' and in the entire temple festival in the last section of 'Passage to India' but in all this divine merriment and super human joy. Forster is liable to find an inter mixture of 'Muddle'; his aesthetic sense is disturbed by the absence of order proportion and from and his religious sense, too, is jolted in the Hindu festival he sees the human spirit is suffering, a 'desperate contortion' in its attempt to ravish the unknown and the individual protagonists of the instinctive life are all with the exception of Ruth Wilcox, to some degree flawed, Stephan is barbarous, Gino cruel, Aziz for all his 'secret-understanding of the heart, suffers an unnecessary – alienation from fielding because he allows his feelings to get the better: sense of evidence. Even Mrs. Moore, who has Mrs. Wilcoxes kind of instinctive wisdom, and whose spirit, like hers, broods as a religious presence over the book after she is dead, loses hold on her vision at a crucial moment, with George Emerson, too, we are told that it is 'touch & go'.

But it can't be said that – Forster is any more satisfied with his protagonists of the life of reason and intellectual culture. Some of them have culture and intelligence without the goodwill, and then in their contemptuous indolence and their rejection of the human, they come near to being ranged with the force of darkness rather than light. Tibby Schlegal betray the blasts to the Wilcox, Philip Harriton could have saved Gino's baby; and Cecil Vyse, in spite of his scorn for many of the Swaston values, is in effect at one with them in his turning away from 'the spirit of life'. Stewart Ansell does not lick goodwill, but there is an obscure in-effectualness about him which affects not only his career but this dealings with his friends. He has his one magnificent – outburst, but apart from this he is oddly silent and withdrawn when Rickie most desperately needs his help. And what of fielding? here clearly there in no absence of capacity to act-when action is needed, and his generous good sense sustains both Adela and Aziz through the major crises of the book. But, like his very much less admirable predecessors. Fielding will 'travel light' if he can, and in particular, he would prefer to escape the complete involvement required either by affection or by what Forster cells the unseen. It is greatly to his credit that he recognizes that—travelling light is less easy as soon as affection is involved; and when he faces its demands whether from Aziz or from Stella, his earlier easy optimism about personal relations fails him. But the religious sensibility which links Aziz, Godbole and Mrs. Moore is beyond his grasp. When Mrs. Moore says, 'I like mysteries but I rather dislike muddle;' Fielding's reply comes sharp, A mystery is muddle; and when he says with the same kind of bluntness... I don't believe in god; the reader, as well as his hearer, is likely to find the words 'too definite and bleak' with all their truth-fullness and impatience with can't, they exclude so much, later when the disaster of the caves opened up not only the depth and bitterness of human animosities but a glimpse of ancient night and the undying worm it self, he is willing to admit that –' perhaps life is a mystery, not a muddle'—but we are told, he had not the apparatus for judging. And although he is aware of the confused Adela and defeated Mrs. Moore, he can't come to terms with it: It belonged to the universe that he had missed or rejected. Hence, when together with Adela he tries to face the tragedy that had over whelmed her, he finds that – sensible, honest and even subtle though they both are, they have no adequate works. In the presence of a displaced worked they are as dwarfs shaking hands.

But suppose that that the two voices, instinct and intelligence, culture and nature, reason and religious insight, culture and nature, reason and religious insight could be combined in one person. Rickie Eliot has something of both; but not enough of either. Helan Schlegal has more force and articulate intelligence than Rickies, but her impulsiveness upsets the balance. But it appears to be Forster's intention that Helen's sister Margaret should serenely combined the two, and that she should be able to connect on a deeper love, – perhaps, than any of the over statement of the book would suggest. – I said earlier that Ruth Wiloox is the only one of the 'instinctive protagonists who is not in adequate, and it could be argued in support of this that it is sufficient for Ruth that, like a poem she should well mean yet she is inadequate in the sense that she needs Margaret to complete her and to realize her potentialities, to turn a diffused radiance into beam of light. Margaret possesses intellectual culture, but it is not this that attracts Ruth to her in fact in the presence of Ruth her clever friends seen like gibbering monkeys. But she has imaginative culture as well, and it is this - admirably summed up by Forster as a 'profound vivacity' which binds the two woman together. I feel obliged to that if I have interpreted Forster's interactions correctly, I am by no means always satisfied that Margaret's action fulfill them, and even after allowing for the fact that she is a person as well as a symbol, and that persons make mistakes, my dissatisfaction remains. But if the attempt to connect the prose and the passion) is only partially successful, she does, I think connect the positive values which Forster has studied on their varying levels, throughout the novels and her quality of mind can perhaps be summed up in a term of Matthew Arnold's imaginative season'.

Now to the simple mind of mention of complication looks like a kind of malice and to the mind under great stress the suggestion of some thing 'behind' the apparent face looks like a call of quietism, like more shilly-shallying and this is the judgment, I think that a great many readers of the most enlightened sort are likely to pass on Forster.

For he stands in a peculiar relation for want of a better word, we may call the liberal tradition, that loose body of middle-class opinion which includes such ideas as progress, collectivism and humanitarianism.

To this tradition Forster has been committed all his novels morally and politically tendentious and always in the liberal direction yet he is deeply, odds with the liberal mind, and while liberal readers can go a long way with Forster, they can seldom go all the way. They can understand him when he attacks the manners and the morals of the British middle-class. When he speaks out for spontaneity of feeling, for the virtues of sexual fulfillment, for the values of intelligence; they go along with him when he speaks against the class system, satirizes soldiers and officials/question the British empire and attack business ethics and the public schools but sooner or later they begin to make reservations and draw back. They suspect Forster not quite playing their game; they feel that he is challenging them as well as what they dislike. And they are right. For all his long commitment to the doctrine of liberalism, Forster is at war with the liberal imagination.

The liberal mind is sure that the human affairs owes it a simple logic; good is good and bad is bad. In can't understand, for it invented and pessimism, but the mood that is the response to good and evil it has not named and court understand, before the idea of good and evil its imagination fails; it can't accept this improbable paradox. This is ironic, for one of the charter documents of liberalism urges the liberal mind to cultivate imagination enough to accept just their improbability and the irony is doubled when we think that how well the great conservative minds have understood what Milton meant—Dr. Johnson and Brurke understood the mystery of the twins; and Mathew Arnold has always been thought the less a liberal for his understanding of them. But we have the liberal connection have always liked to play the old intellectual game of antagonistic principles. It is an attractive game because it gives us the sensation of twinkling and its first rule is that of one of two opposed principle is wrong, the other is necessarily right. Forster will not play this game; or, rather, he plays it only to work it.

This indifference to the commonplaces of liberal thought makes the very texture of Forster's novels and appeared in the first of them. The theme of 'Where angles fear to Tread' is the violent opposition between British respectability and a kind of pagan and masculine integration. D.H. Lawrence, who worked something in this area gave us many characters like Forster's Gino and Cardella, characters like Gino, was cruel or like Gino indifferent to the higher and romantic emotions but here Lawrence always stopped; from this points on all his efforts went, to intensifying his picture and by this he double gained as against Forster, in sheer coercive power. For the poor, lost, respectable British people, Gino may serve as the embodiment of masculine and pager principle but Forster knows that he is also coarse, dull, vain pretensions, facilely polite and very much taken with the charm of respectability.

In "A Room with a View" to take another example which leads us to make the typical Liberal discovery that Miss Bartlett, the poor relation who thinks she is acting form duty, is really action from a kind of malice she has been trying to recruit the awakened heroine into "the armies of the benighted, who follows neither the heart nor the brain". But Forster does not stop at this conventionality, even though in 1908, it was not quite so conventional. For when the heroine at last fulfills her destiny. Then Mi ss Bertlet who marries the man she had unconsciously loved, she comes to perceive that she had really desired the union. And we have been prepared for this demonstration of the something still for their behind' the apparent by the action of the tolerant and enlightened clergyman, Mr. Beebe, who has ceased to be the angel of light and has set himself against the betrothal.

Forster's insistence of the double turn, on the something else that lies behind is something taken for tolerance; but although it often suggests forgiveness it almost as often makes the severest judgments. And even when it suggests forgiveness it does not spring so much form gentleness of heart as from respect for two facts co-existing form the neural realism and understand the one apple tarred. Forster can despise of Gerald of 'The Longest Journey' because Gerald is a prig and a bully but he can invest Gerald's death with a kind of primitive dignity, telling us of the maid servant who weeps, 'they had not liked Gerald but he was a man, they were woman, he had died and after Gerald's death he can given Agnes Pembroke her moment of nobility only to peruse her implacability for her genteel brutality.

So much moral realism is rare enough to be kind of surprise and Forster likes to work with surprise mind. Gerald died that after noon; is the beginning of a chapter which follows immediately upon a description full of superabundant life we have to stand unusually for back, from Forster's character not to be startled when they turn about and the peculiar pleasure to be had from his books is that of a judicious imperturbability. He is always shocking us by removing the heroism of her heroes and heroines; in 'A passage to India' Mrs. Moore of whom we had expected high actions, lets herself he sent away from the trial which hertestimony would have been crucial; Cyril opposed official ideas, himself become official when he is successful and married; and Aziz can't keep to his role of the sensitive and enlightened native. Let us not deceive ourselves, Forster seems to say, it is with just each frailties as Mrs. Moore and Mr. Fielding, and with and for such unregeneracies as Dr. Aziz that the problem of, let us say, India must be solved. The moment of any man's apparent grace are few, any man may have them and their effects are not easily to be calculated. It is on a helter skelter distribution of grace that Forster pins. What hopes he has; but for yeers after 'A Passage to India', it is skill his latest novel he has had the increasing sense of possible doom.

Forster has been able to deal so well with the idea of class. The liberal mind has the time spoken much of this idea but has failed to believe in it. The modern liberal believes in categories and wage-scales and calls these class. Forster knows better and in 'Howards End' shows the conflicting truth of ideas—but on the one hand class is character, soul and destiny, and that on the other hand class is not finally determining. He knows that class may be truly represented only by struggle and contradiction, not by description, and preferably by moral struggle and a single person. When D.H. Lawrence wrote to Forster that he had made a nearly deadly mistake glorifying those business people in 'Howards End.' Business is no good, he was indulging his own case taste for the unconditioned. It led him to read Forster in accurately and it led him to make that significant shift from 'business people' to 'business'. But Forster who is too wordly to suppose that we can judge class conditioned action until we make a hypothetical deduction of the subjects essential humanity. It is exactly because Forster can judge the 'business people' as he does, and because he can judge to lower class without sentimentality that he deal firmly and intelligently with his own class, and this is middle in Howards End- and the nearly allegorical reconsideration is rather forced—than, in speaking of class, clear ideas are perhaps the sign of ignorance, middle the sign of true knowledge; surely Howards End stands with 'our Mutual friend' and the 'princess casamassina' as one of the great comment on class struggle.

The great thing Forster has been able to learn from his attachment to tradition and from his sense of the past is his belief in the present. He has learned not to be what most of us areeschatological. Most of us consciously or unconsciously, are discontented with the nature rather than with the use of the human faculty; deep in our assumption lies the hope and the belief that the humanity will ends his career by developing virtues which will be admirable exactly because now we can't conceive them. The past has been a weary failure, the present can't matter, for it is but a step forward for the final judgment; we look to the future when the best of the works of man will deem but the futile and slightly disgusting twitching of primeval creatures: thus in the name of a superior and contemptuous posterity, we express ours self-hatred and our desire for power.

This is a moral and historical error into which Forster never falls; his wrote work indeed, is an implied protest against it. The very relaxation of his style, its colloquial unpretentiousness, is a mark of his acceptance of the human fact as we know it now. He is content with the human possibility and content with its limitation. The way of human action of course do not satisfy him, but he does not believe these are any new virtues to be discover not by becoming better, he says, but by ordering and distributing his native goodness can man live as befits him.

It seems to me, might well be called worldliness, this acceptance of man in the world without the sentimentality of cynicism and without the sentimentality of rationalism. Forster is that remarkably rare being, a naturalist, whose naturalism is positive and passionate, not negative, passive and apologistic for man's nature. He accepts the many things the liberal imagination likes to putout of sight. He can accept, for example, not only the reality but power of death;

"Death destroys a man, the idea of death saves him."[21]

And the fine scene in 'The Longest Journey' in which Rickie forces the Agnes to 'mind' the death of Gerald is a criticism not only of the British fear of emotion but also of liberalism's incompetence before tragedy. To Forster, as to Black, naturalism suggests not the invalidity and strength.

It is so worldly; indeed that he believes that ideas for his service and that not for his worship. In 1939, when war was certain and the talk ran so high and loose about democracy that it was hard to know what was being talked about, Forster remarked with easy simplicity of a man in his own house.

"So two cheers for democracy; one because of it admits variety and two because it permits criticism. Two cheers are quite enough: there is no occasion to give there. Only love the beloved Republic deserves that."

He is so worldly that he always felt that his nation belonged to him. He has always known that we can't love anything bigger until we first love and so it has been easy for him to seek of his love for his country with whose faults he has never ceased to quarrel; and now he has no void to fill up with the acrid nationalism that literary man too often feel called upon to express in a time of crisis. He is one of the thinking people who were never led by thought to suppose they could be more than human and who, in bad times, wil! not become less.

References

1. Forster, E.M., "Abinger Harvest ", 'The Consolation of History' p. 191.
2. Crews, Fredricks C., E.M. Forster: 'The Perils of Humanism' (Princeton Univ. Press, 1962), p. 24.
3. Forster, E.M., Two Cheers of Democracy, The Menace to Freedom, p. 21.
4. Liddell, Robert, A Treatise on the Novel (London, 1947), p. 60.
5. Forster, E.M., Two Cheers for Democracy, Gide and Georg, p. 233.
6. *Ibid.,* p. 80.
7. Forster, E.M. : Abinger Harvest, Liberty in England, p. 79.
8. *Ibid.,* p. 85.
9. *Ibid.,* p. 285.
10. Forster, E.M., Two Cheers for Democracy, What I Believe, p. 85.
11. Aspect of the Novel, p. 136.
12. Forster, E.M., Abinger Harvest, My Wood, p. 36.
13. *Ibid.,* p. 72.
14. Trilling, Lionall, The Liberal Imagination (London, 1951), p. 15.
15. Crews, Frederick, C., E.M Forster: The Perils of Humanism, p. 6.
16. Kettle, Arnold: E.M.Forster: A Passage to India: An Introduction to the English Novel, Vol. 2 (London, 1953), p. 153.

17. Forster, E.M., Two Cheers for Democracy, p. 136.
18. Thomson, Gh, Thematic Symbol in *A Passege to India*, Vol. 7, 1961, p. 61.
19. *Howards End*, p. 72.
20. Forster, E.M., *Two Cheers for Democracy, What I Belive*, p. 94.
21. *Howards End*, p. 46.

5

East-West Encounter

Forster's "A Passage to India" is a major document as a piece of anti-imperialist propaganda, polemic against British rule in India. There are the civil servants outwards bound for India, who bought the novel as suitable reading for their voyage, only to throw their copies over board angrily, when then they discovered the contents. If they did so, they were behaving more like the Indian civil servants of popular caricature than do Forster's own characters. They represent the short haired executive type obtuse, egotistic, unscrupulous, cowards, spiritually, self-deceiving successful.

Forster was one of the first writers to challenge the complacent imperial assumption of the British ruling class that it ruled India for India's own good. Instead, Forster sees the British rule as a corrupting influence on both the ruler and the ruled. However, Forster's criticism is based on ethical rather than political convictions. Forster's condemnation of British rule in India ultimately rests on a deep humanistic belief in the "sanctity of personal relationship": Forster was pained to see that close personal relationship that ought to have existed between Indians and the British were corrupted by Imperial rule due to its cruel division of humanity into the rulers and the ruled, white and coloured.

In "A Passage to India" Forster provides a complex study of relationships individual and communal, between the

English and the Indians. The earlier part of the book is concerned primarily with showing the relations between the rulers and the ruled. Chandrapore is two towns. the native section and the British civil station. Forster noted the contrast: "The civil station shares nothing with the city except the over arching sky."[1]

In their dealings with Indians, the British, as a class, operate only at the level of political and social duty. In other words, their relationship with Indians is those of the political and social roles they play. In this, of course, they are eminently successful. The ethics of the ruling class are dutiful and serious, the Anglo-Indians rulers have a deep sense of rational justice, they are distrustful of mysticism and lethargy, they even feel that their role has been indicative in their situation. Rony Heaslop puts the case of the British rulers when he says: "We're out here to do justice and keep the peace we are not pleasant in India, and we don't intend to be pleasant. We're something more important to do."[2]

Insofor as it goes, this is a convincing description of the venal and shifty ways of Indians in their contact with the British. As Lionell Trilling observes: "Although the Indians are conceived in sympathy and affection, they are conceived with these emotions alone, and although all of them have charm, none of them has dignity, they touch one's heart, but they never impress us."[3]

In their passive response to a long period of humiliating rule as also to the hostile landscape in which they are placed, the Indians have naturally lost all dignity. Their personalities do not have the firm outlines that the British so cherish. The Indians consequently appear as lethargic and emotionally shoddy. Towards the British, they behave in general like rebellious adolescents. They are petulant and defiant at one time and at another pathetically dependent on the British for kindness. They are anxious to integrate themselves to their British masters and yet they are also nervously defensive of their loyalty to the rules.

But all these defects, Forster takes pains to show, are the effect of the humiliating and undignifying rule of the

British over the Indians. Generation of the subjection have degraded the personalities of the Indians and have made them what they are unreliable, childish and suspicious. However, the British themselves are not free from vices either. If the Indians think collectively out of fear and hatred, the British in turn behave as a herd, rigidly cutting themselves off from the Indians. They have build around themselves a rigid barrier of conventions of rank and position, and feeling safe and superior behind this fence of conventions, they look down upon the Indians outside with contempt and disdain. Anglo-Indians rules have become, as a class, crude, arrogant and insensitive. Fearful of the primitive Indians outside they always feel of sticking together, or keeping in step with other in order not to fall behind the herd. When Fielding tries to break away from the Anglo-Indians on the issue of Aziz's arrest, Mr. Bryde, the typical British Burra Sahib advises him:

> "We shall all have to hang together, old man, I'm afraid at a time like this there's no room for well personal views. The man who doesn't toe the line is lost."[4]

All this indicates that it is because the British do not care to understand the true nature of India and the Indians that their rule is so unsuccessful, their contact with the Indians is so limited and meaningless. Unlike other critics of British rule, Forster, does not question the right of the British to be Indian. His main criticism of the British rule is that it is an order of force and will, not of love and understanding "what is needed" says Aziz: "is goodwill, more goodwill and more goodwill"; Forster seems to suggest that this is the answer to the problem of British rule in India. Wilfred Stone remarks:

> "The ugly realities underlying the presence of the British in India are not even glanced at, and the issue are handled as though they could be solved on the surface level of personal intercourse and individual behaviour."[5]

As a study of race relations, 'A passage to India' provides a pitiless exposure of the evil of the British rule in India, the degrading effects it had on both the rulers and the ruled. The earlier part of the novel is concerned with showing the wide gulf between the English and the Indians. As is shown in the very first chapter of the novel, Chandrapore is two towns, the English civil station and the native section, the one having nothing to do with the other. "Is it possible to be friend with an Englishman?"[6] The Indian ask the question and Forster's answer in the novel is a clear one—as long as the English remain unfeeling, proud and autocratic towards the Indians. In their dealing with Indians, the British as a class, operate only at the level of political and social duty. In this of course, they are eminently successful Forster is at pains to point out the achievement of the British rule. The ethics of the ruling class are dutiful and serious; the Anglo Indian ruler have a deep sense of rational justice, they are distrustful of mysticism and lethargy; they even feel that their role has been vindicated in their situation.

The most frightening expression of this hard feeling is of course when the largest members of them are gathered together in their club. At the instance of the new comers, Mrs. Moore and Adela, the local Britishers throw the party inviting the Indians—it is to be a bridge party, bridging the gulf between the English and the Indians. But of course the gap is not 'bridged', because the Anglo-Indians as a group are simply not interested in talking to the Indians they themselves have invited. And when some of them do go towards the Indians and talk to them, it is with condescension so severe as to paralyze whatever contact they have made. The up shot of all this that the Indians who have come innocently and eagerly to earth the goodwill of their British rulers are humiliated in the most indecent manner. In this sort of attitude towards Indians one can see the Britishers contempt and hatred of anything Indian, but one must not miss the fact that this revulsion against the Indians is also due to the secret fear of the Indians race from whose muddled way they want to protect themselves as well as they can —"one's only hope was to hold sternly aloof,"[7] as one of them puts it. The attitude of sacred revulsion explains the efforts of the British to band themselves together. There is a hysteria in this hard feeding. On critical situation, as the case of Adela's experience in the caves, the mass hysteria of the Anglo-Indians makes them shriek for revenge against Indians for harming their innocent girl 'fresh from England'. Their collective concern, as we see in the trail is not justice for Adela, but to achieve the utmost humiliation of the Indians. Forster show how their mass hysteria can, on critical situations, lead them towards how uncontrollable evil.

However, as Forster shows in the novel, the Indians are not free from vices either. While Forster is sympathetic towards the Indians, he does not spare them from his satire and shows them as being unreliable, suspicious and childish. In their passive response to a long period of humiliating rule as also to the hostile landscape in which they are place, the Indians have naturally lost all dignity. There personalities do not have the firm outlines that the British so cherish. The Indians consequently appear as lethargic and emotionally shoddy. Towards the British, they behave in general like rebellious adolescents. They are petulant and defiant at one time and at another pathetically dependent on the British for the kindness. They are anxious to integrate themselves to their British masters and yet they are also nervously defensive of their loyalty to the rules. However, Forster has the perspicacity to realize that the undignified behaviour of the Indians is the result of their humiliating subjection to the imperial rule. On the other hand, when prejudices are set aside by the ruling Britishers, genuine friendship to be shown is possible. On this level at least Forster's answer to the racial problem is; "Goodwill, more goodwill and even goodwill."[8]

The British officials take bribes and do not do the work. We came to know from Mahmoud Ali:

"When we poor black take bribes, we perform what

we are bribed to perform and the law discovers us in consequence. The English take and do nothing."[9]

In 'A Passage to India' we can easily see the intense encounter between the East—(India) and the West (Britain). They regarded themselves as gods and did not—establish any rapport with the Indians. They had a feeling of superiority of their race and culture. Their public school education had taught them to distrust the emotions and to care only reason in all their dealings. They had no sympathy with the Indians.

One main question that Forster present in this novel is weather it is possible for Indians to be friendly with the Englishman. Mr. Fielding for instance, wants to be friendly with Aziz, but it is very difficult. "Not, that is, till the English have been driven out of India, when a friendship based on equality rather than imperialism will be possible."[10] The failure of this connection between the British and the Indians is a running theme in the novel.

Socially they kept apart from the subject people. Their club was their sacred shrine and they did not want Indians to mix with them there. Even the wealthy Nawab Bahadur was not welcome in their club. Their racial prejudice was summed up by one of them who said, "I have never known anything but disaster result when English people and Indians attempt to be intimate socially, Intercourse, yes. Courtesy, by all means, Intimacy never, never.[11]

References

1. Forster, E.M. : *A Passage to India* (London Edward Arnold 1924), p. 32.
2. *Ibid.*, p. 102.
3. Trilling, Lionall: *E. M. Forster*, Norfold, Conn. New Directions Book 1943, p. 202.
4. Forster, E.M. : *A Passage to India* (London Edward Arnold 1924), p. 184.
5. Stone, Wilfred: Cave and the Mountain; *A Study of E. M. Forster*, Oxford University Press, 1966, p. 48.

6. Forster, E. M. : *A Passage to India* (London Edward Arnold 1924), p. 92.
7. *Ibid.*, p. 162.
8. *Ibid.*, p. 221.
9. *Ibid.*, p. 108.
10. *Ibid.*, p. 224.
11. *Ibid.*, p. 172.

6

Plot Character and Technique

(A) Technique and Point of View

The novel, considered primarily as an instrument of instruction and entertainment in the eighteenth century, became towards the close of the nineteenth century the most important art-form. The narrative devices of the novel- "handling of the action, development of characters, presentation of ideas and focus of narration"[1] – were developed by the English novelists in the eighteenth century, whereas the perfection of the technique of the English novel was achieved by later writers, Wilkie Collins recognized the importance of form in fiction, form became dominant in George Moore and especially in Henry James, George Meredith built his novels round a theme, and there was "a progressive development in this respect, through Moore, James, Conrad and E.M. forester."[2]

The three essential ingredients of fiction, according to Wright Morris in *The Territory Ahead*, are: first, the raw material which is the subject-matter of the novel; secondly technique, which is the method of collecting the raw material; thirdly, the shaping imagination, of "the transforming technician which transforms the "illusive facts" into "a fiction of permanence", Wright Morris writes "technique and raw material are essential to both the study and the laboratory."[3]

The conquest of matter is possible only if the artist has a complete understanding and mastery of his technique. (4)

Life presents the subject-matter to the novelist, the most intriguing problem of the writer's craft, according to Erich Auerbach in Mimesis, is the one which is connected with the portrayal of objective reality, the creative mind of the author gives to the material of life a definite form, a neat design, and a clear pattern. Life, however, is not "static" but changing, and the form of the novel, too, varies. When in the ideas, experiences, moods, attitudes change, freshness can be imparted to the material of life by the creative artist.

"The history of fiction, its pursuit of that chimera we describe as reality, is a series of imaginative triumphs made possible through technique" on another life. Art, if it is to have value, "must always be renewed"[5] the creative value of art depends on "surprise" and also on "the freshness of the presentment". The novel is significant because at the center it is the imaginative vision of the novelist which binds the different parts and gives meaning to life. The totality of all the elements that go to make a work of art the story, the plot, the people, the social setting, the structure, and the pattern in the novel, is determined to some extent by the vision of the novelist "the singleness of vision"[6] according to Virginia Woolf; "insight" and "clarity of mind", according to Elizabeth drew; "truth", according to D.S. savage; the novelist's view of life and his "imaginative comprehension" and "penetration".

"Yet if there is one gift more essential to a novelist than another, it is the power of combination—the single vision".

According to Dr. Arnold Kettle; "all-embracing vision"[7] according to R.A. Scott-James; and the writer's "bias" according to W. Somerset Maugham, form is inevitable when the vision of the novelist shapes the material of life. Structure, in fact, is the external shape which the living idea of the novelist takes. It is "form" which possesses completeness, unity, and coherence. Form and content, according to Ralph Fox, are neither "separate" nor "passive entities" . The writer's outlook on life is "his touchstone for reality" and is his "way of perceiving and knowing the real world"[8] form is "the expression of a thought — organism" and is "the objective order that has been imposed on matter by the mind". As a result of the novelist's view-point, all the separate parts are fused into an organic whole. The novelist's point of view gives to the matter a formalized neatness, an intellectual solidity, and an emotional unity.

Dorothy van Chent, in the English Novel, writes that "technique" has undergone many changes and it is necessary to discuss the matter of techniques in fiction of each novel[9] —as a work of art—is to be properly evaluated. The study of the technique of the novel" enlarges our understanding" and at the same time it "deepens our pleasure". A. A. Mendilow, in time and the novel, writes that "one should not talk of the technique of novels". (10) The novel, as a work of art, is created and it should be judged by its own rules. In Aspects of the novel, Forster writes:

> Apart from schools and influences and fashions, there has been a technique in English fiction, and this does alter from generation to generation.[11]

D.S. Savage regards technique as the device of method which particularly suits a writer and his subject-matter,[12] the artist has to create a technique for his particular purpose.

Technique, however, in subservient to vision, Mark Schorer on the other hand, regards "technique" as "discovery" in the Rhetoric of Fiction, Wayne C. Booth writes that technique is important because it enables the author to control the subject-matter, the form of the novel and his reader's response. The novelist succeeds in his mission if, by the technique of non-didactic fiction, he moves his readers "into a new order of perception and experience".[13] Thus when the work is completed everything becomes "intrinsic". Technique—whether it is defined as "process", or "discovery", or "rhetoric" — is "instinctive" and its value as a shaping instrument has to be acknowledged. Elizabeth Drew, therefore, regards all the methods, used by the novelist, as good provided they "are effective for his own purpose".[14]

According to Miriam Allott, there are four types of structure in fiction depending on the role of the novelist—the novelist as a commentator, as analyst, as a sage, and as a prophet. As a commentator, the novelist is "inclusive" and he employs comedy, irony, and satire as the instruments of his "critical strategy". He attacks the conventions and the pretensions of society and separates falsehood from truth by the device of the double vision, one eye turning on society and the other on seif. As an analyst of individual feelings and emotions, he is " exclusive" and he dramatizes the center of consciousness and makes use of tragic experience and the stream of consciousness technique. He has a highly developed sense of form and his theme is the tragic theme of self-betrayal. As a sage, he combines "the inclusive writer's uneconomical prodigality and the exclusive writer's feeling for pattern", and finally, as a prophet, he is a symbolist whose poetic imagination expresses itself, "through symbols and sustained metaphors". The novel assumes the form of the comedy of manners when it becomes a criticism of the English middle-class and its social morels. It assumes the form of fantasy when, with the searchlight of imagination, he illumines the ordinary material of life. It assumes the form of prophecy when it deals with the universal values. The novel becomes a criticism of society, and an exposure of its shams and pretensions. On its destructive side, Forster's critical spirit unmasks hypocrisy; on the level of creation, his creative power focuses our attention on the worth of the true self of man. On the level of social comedy, the novels of Forster are concerned with society and show his spirit of criticism at work on manners, morals and mores of the English middle-class. On the level of fantasy and prophecy, they establish contact with self by rejecting worldliness, self-consciousness, and will. On the level of symbolism, Forester's poetic vision of life is something beyond the grasp of cold reason.

Forster, in an interview at King's College, Cambridge, on the evening of June 20th, 1952, stated that—"the novelist"

Forster thinks, "should always settle, when he starts what his major event is to be".[15]

It is not necessary that all the important steps in the plot must be present in the original connection, but there must be "some major object towards which one is to approach".[16] Forster speaks of "antitheses" in his novels but in "Arctic Summer", though he got his antithesis between "the civilized man" and "the heroic man", he had not settled his major event and since the atmosphere of "Arctic Summer", lacked density, concentration could not take place and an event could not be engendered.[17] That is why "Arctic Summer" emains a fragment. In each of the five published novels of Forster, the plot is based on "antithesis". For he is confronted with division: the two types of character, the "crustaceans" and the "vitalists"; the two types of being, the social being and the imaginative being; the kinds of society, the "Great Society" and the" Little Society", the two sorts of heart, the "developed" and the "undeveloped"; and the two forms of spirit, the masculine and the feminine. It is by means of contrast that Forster has been able to give to his novels a simple, and significant form.

Forster's understanding of life is based on his personal outlook. Confronted with the material of life, Forster tries to seek" a convenient vantage post" so that he can look at it without any obstruction. Forster, in 'Where Angle Fear to Trend', tries to remain detached and watches the spectacle of life critically and dispassionately. In the projected image of himself in the person of Philip Herriton, he stands aloof from humanity. Philip Herriton is an academician, an aesthete, and a humorist. His detachment from life is the result of his intellectual snobbery. It is the aim of Forster to keep himself at a distance, and survey life from the mid-point position. Like Philip Herriton, he is untouched by life; he is only an observer and he feels superior to it. Forster's point of view, is, perhaps, similar to the point of view of Philip Herriton who says that life to him is just a "spectacle" and he seems, "fated to pass through the world without colliding with it or moving it".[18] Miss Abbott who, from the mid-point of view, is able to discern the boundaries of sorrow with infinite pity saves Philip, Miss Abbott. When Gino stumbles and clings to her like a child, seems to Philip like a goddess. She, at the mid-point of view, is detached as well as attached because she is able to discern human suffering and is full of love and compassion for those who suffer. She looks young because of emotion and old because of wisdom. In the end, she is completely transformed for she has no concern with refinement or unrefinement. It is Miss Abbott who reveals to Philip the indestructible nature of the true self of man. Philip, too, is lifted to the same height and he becomes her worshipper. Forster selects the mid-point of view because from this post of observation he can discern the littleness of life and the unfading glory of the transcendental reality. It is in *A Passage to India* that Forster has gained an insight at a high level of intuition and the author's view becomes a reliable commentary on people who are "sensible, honest, even subtle". Fielding and Miss Quested are dwarfs for they have seen "their own gestures from an immense height -dwarfs talking, shaking hands and assuring each other that they stood on the same footing of insight".[19] The author at the mid-point gains a correct prospective. From the exalted point of view, Forster enables us to see that physical reality is incomplete without the superhuman reality. The story, according to Forster, has a value when it "adds something because of its connection with a voice"[20] The Forsterian voice detached, solitary, compassionate, and prophetic — is important in the novels of Forster. Forster may shift his attention from character to character but his point of view remains unaltered and "still maintains its control" over the characters. Forster views his characters from a remove, and the focus he chooses is the basis of his "irony", of his "double vision", and of "the unique accents of the Forsterian voice".[21]

The novels of Forster, according to Peter Burra, are the "most distinguished pieces of craftsmanship" and rhythm is the quality, which gives unity to the novel. Rhythm implies the use of phrases and images to link the separate parts of the novel, with the additional function of dramatic irony and symbolism. Irony is an important aspect of Forster's point of view. Forster, like Jane Austen, is a master of a subtle and devastatingly powerful irony. Irony is primarily a method of "comprehension". It is a stylistic device, a point of view, a moral focus, a subtle means of expression, an illuminating, a satirical thrust, and a manifestation of the writer's state of mind. At its best, irony is a tone of "seeming seriousness" and inward laughter; it "insinuate, without a word of moral, aesthetic, or any other kind of criticism".[22] Direct attack looks clumsy and inartistic. On the other hand, a feigned tone to seriousness and seeming gravity is highly amusing and revealing. Irony is based on contrast/the contrast between virtue and meanness. We are amused at the self-betrayal of characters. Irony exposes falsehood, which exists in many forms and appears in varied disguises. It is, therefore, a safety valve through which the powerful steam of moral indignation escapes. Subtle irony is a clever device, which is based on hint, insinuation and indirect attack. It is an oblique method but it helps in the comprehension of reality, and in the true understanding of character. Through the use of irony, a situation can be made to appear absurd, ludicrous, and even grotesque. Irony does not state. It reveals character and the meaning of life. It can be merry, sarcastic and amusing on the one hand; on the other hand, it can be indignant, bitter, and cynical. Forster's irony is a mixture of banter and cynicism, jest and seriousness. It is with added to weighty and serious matter. With the help of irony, the novelist is able to make indignant thrusts and amusing digs at human pride, selfishness, meanness, and hypocrisy. Mrs. Herriton, Harriet Herriton, Cecil Vyse, Mr. Beebe, Cuthbert Eager, Henry Wilcox, Mrs. Failing, Herbert Pembroke, and other conventional characters are unmasked and ridiculed. Forster's approach to social conventions and moral standards is critical and satirical. In fact, Forster believes in a discipline, which is evolved from within and not imposed from without. He believes in an order which is based on inner conviction and faith and not on external authority. Irony, as an apparatus of exposure, and a sharp weapon of criticism, has been effectively used by Forster in his novels. Doctrines, rigid rules, ethical code, sexual morality, morality social taboos, pretended virtue hypocritical behaviour, unhealthy prudery, and self-deception are ridiculed by Forster in his novels. In his novels, Forster criticizes the imperfect theories of bourgeois morality by placing them along the real and ugly facts of human life—greed, cruelty, vulgarity and spitefulness. Through his use of subtle irony, Sawston emerges as a place of moral obtuseness, hypocrisy, pretended virtue, conceit and cruelty. The social types in his novels are shown moving round and round the tether of social conventions and taboos. Their lives are shown as meaningless and purposeless. Irony, therefore, in the novels of Forster is a point of view which brings out the contrast between falsehood and truth, appearance and reality, hypocrisy and sincerity, self -betrayal and awareness of self. Forster's irony reveals the absurdity of social behaviour seen in the light of motives. It undermines all material values, pretensions, affectations, pride, self-important and egotism. Forster's use of irony can be seen in his novels. Mr. Kingcroft carrying "a foot-warmer by both ends, as if it was a tea-tray"; Mrs. Herriton's complete change of front of her attitude to Lilia's baby, Mr. Beebe's behaviour when he learns that Lucy has decided to marry George Emerson, Henry Wilcox's proposal to Margaret; and the gestures of Fielding and Adela — as seen by them from an immense height — as of "dwarfs". Irony, in fact, helps Forster in "deflating the heroic status of the characters and making them appear futile." It "infiltrates its way into all situations,"[23] and undermines the importance of people, action, and human life as in the dinner scene in 'Where, Angels Fear to Tread.'

The imaginative vision of Forster, springing from the subconscious depths, is his unique perception of the meaning of life. The unconscious, according to Walter Allen, is, perhaps, "knowable only through the symbol". The symbol is a revelation of the deeper reality hidden beneath appearance. It expresses the author's state of mind and his imaginative vision of life. It explores different levels of reality.

In fact, intuition—the flash of revelation and the moment of intense vision can be expressed symbolically through imagery. The appeal of the symbol is not rational but poetic. The function of art is to discover a technique by means of which the artist is able to "seize the inner reality of existence",[24] and, at the same time, express the "nuances of thought and emotion which have long existed as part of our own inner life". The artist, through the use of symbols, tries to express "the elusive states of soul and to rescue it from the magic cave of the subconscious".[25] The artist's vision explores the interior catches the nuances of feeling and rescues the true self from the grip of individual consciousness. Through the symbol he perceives truth, comprehends reality, accepts intrinsic value, and rejects falsehood. The symbol becomest'effective when it is realistic."[26] The creative artist draws his images from scenes, places, characters, objects, incidents and experiences, and they become alive when they reveal the deeper reality. The conventional symbols, however, loose the freshness, the wholeness and the significance of the simple images. Forster, in 'Where Angels Fear to Tread,' writes that the symbol, the visible form is inadequate when the theme is great:

> "Philip looked away, as he sometimes looked away from the great pictures where visible forms suddenly became inadequate for the things they have shown to us."[27]

Forster's view of symbolism is recorded by P.N. Furbank and F.J.H. Haskell in 'The Paris Review' Interviews—the tree at Howards End, "was symbolical; it was the genius of the house."[28] His use of rhythm—the "easy", the "difficult", and "the expanding symbol"—has been discussed in detail by J.K. Johnstone in the Bloomsbury Group, and also by James McConkey in The Novels of E.M. Forster. Forster, in 'Aspects of the Novel,' defines rhythm as "repetition plus variation"; the phrase of Vinteuil, according to Forster, has "a life of its own and it stitches" Proust's book together from the inside, and towards the establishment of beauty and the ravishing of the reader's memory."[29] Forster has made use of "rhythm" in his novels: the violets growing in rich profusion in the little wood near Monteriano and the killing of the baby in an accident in that wood, the washing of the baby and Gino resting his head on the breast of Miss Abbott, in 'Where Angels Fear to Tread'; the three Italians who sympathize with Lucy, in 'A Room with a view'; the suggestive power of Orion and the Roman road level-crossing in *The Longest Journey*; the last two movements of the fifth symphony and the hay symbol in Howards End; and, finally, the wasp and the phrase: "Then you are an Oriental" in 'A Passage to India.'

The deeper reality which constantly haunts the mind of Forster is hidden, beneath the objective reality. The inner reality cannot be expressed except through music. In an address "The Raison d' Etre of Criticism in the Arts' delivered at a symposium on Music at Harvard University in 1947", Forster said:

> .... Music is the deepest of the arts and deep beneath the arts....[30]

Fiction, according to Forster, "is likely to find its nearest parallel in music."[31] Forster is in favour of an art, which, like the art of music, is coherent rather than, episodic, concentrated rather than diffuse, deep rather than superficial, harmonious rather than disorderly, significant rather than meaningless. Music stirs the deepest chords of the human soul, enables the individual to liberate himself from the shackles of time and space to lead a larger existence. In the novel 'Where Angels Fear to Tread', Forster describes the seen with great gusto, The theatre murmurs like a hive of happy bees. Miss Abbott, too falls into the spirit of universal joy that pervades the theatre:

> "Miss Abbott fell into the spirit of the thing. She, too, chatted and laughed and

> applauded and encored, and rejoiced in the existence of beauty, As for Philip, he forgot himself as well as his mission.[32]

Lucy Honeychurch finds daily life dull, but when she opens the piano she enters a more solid world than the world in which she lives:

> "The kingdom of music is not the kingdom of this world: it will accept these whom breeding, intellect and culture have alike rejected.[33]

Music ensures man joy in the midst of suffering, Samuel Butler liked the music of Handel and Beethoven, Forster, likewise, appreciates the music of Beethoven:

> "Beethoven is so usually simple and Direct in his appeal......."[34]
> Music clarifies the vision of Lucy Honeychurch:
> "Lucy never, know her desires so clearly as after music."[35]

Music evokes memories and emotions, which are real. Forster, in 'A Room With a View,' quotes Samuel Butler when he makes Mr. Emerson say:

> " Life ", wrote a friend of mine, "is a public performance on the violin, in which you must learn the instrument as you go along".[36]

The easy type of rhythm is simple but the difficult type of rhythm is meaningful. The fifth symphony of Beethoven achieves completeness "mainly (though not entirely) by the relation between the three big blocks of sound which the orchestra has been playing."[37] In Howards End, Forster describes the effect of music, Beethoven scatters the goblins of panic and emptiness and brings back the "gusts of splendour":

"He brought back the gusts of splendour,
The heroism, the youth, the magnificence
Of life and of death, and, amid vast.

Rearing of a superhuman joy, he led his fifth symphony to its confusion.[38] In *A Passage to India*, the song sung by Godbole is meaningful:

"His thin voice rose, and gave out one sound
after another, At times there seemed rhythm,
at times there was the illusion of the Western
melody. But the ear, baffled repeatedly,
soon lost any clue, and wandered in a maze
of noises, none harsh of unpleasant, none
Intelligible. It was the song of an unknown bird.[39]

The effect of Godbole's song on the servants is miraculous for its appeal is direct:

"Only the servants understood it. They began
to whisper to one another. The man who was
gathering water chestnut came naked out of the
tank, his lips parted with delight, disclosing
his scarlet tongueo.[40]

Music is harmony for it unites all the discordant elements In a single impression which is complete. Forster, in the last section—"Temple"—of *A Passage to India*, has described the effect and function of music—"Tukaram, Tukaram Chorus:

Music there was, but from so many sources
that the sum-total was untrammeled. The braying
banging crooning melted into a single mass which trailed
round the palace
before joining the thunder.[41]

The novels of Forster are in touch with the outer life as well as the inner life and vision and realism co-exist in Forster's work.[42]

—

The artist reveals his personality through style. Whatever, the tendency of the artist may be, whether classical or romantic, the final impression he leaves on the mind of the reader is indelible. The writer's personality remains visible unless he conceals his personality altogether by a smoke screen which comes in between the writer and the reader. His distinct personality is discernible from his comments. His outlook, and his manner of writing. The novel, too, like any other art, acquires a distinct character because of the personal touch of the novelist. He betrays himself by a remark, a comment, a distinct turn of thought, an odd phrase, a peculiar tone, and a preference for certain words, which are repented. It is the writer's vision that brings about the fusion of form and content, meaning and material, subject-matter and thought. The novelist has to borrow words for the expression of his thought and feeling; and, since the writer has a distinct personality and a unique individual vision, he has his own way of choosing words and constructing sentences. The mode of expression is individualistic and varies from writer to writer. Style is the mode of expression and it consist of several ingredients—thought, feeling, imagination, inner convictions, basic faith and outlook. These ingredients leaven the work of an artist and give life and vitality to it. Style is vital to fiction and is imperative, as H.J. Oliver says in the 'Art of E.M. Forster', if the author's personality is to be an important element in the whole.[43] Style, on the case of Forster's novels is one quality "that is never forgotten." Forster's style is important for it bears the hallmark of a personality that is sensitive, sympathetic, tolerant, independent, unyielding to conventions, free, whimsical and elusive. Forster's style, according to Trilling, sometime becomes "arch, whimsical and feminine",[44] and at times ironic, indignant and vehement. At other times, it becomes subjective, imaginative, highly concentrated, and sometimes quite intimate. When he in carried away by moral fervour, it becomes rhetorical. The style of Forster varies from light and pointed irony to serious and profound thought, from poetic and tender manner of writing to pompous oratory, from explosive mood to the gentle attitude, and from remarkable vigour to sensitized feeling Thus it varies, according to the mood and the theme and the situation, and it is the measuring rod of the strength and the weakness of his mind. Forster has not included style in "Aspects of the Novel." Nevertheless, he has made references here and there of the writer's personality which reveals itself in the pages of the book and survives. Forster in against mechanical writing and clumsy style. He is in favour of humour, jest, irony and sarcasm. Criticism has been made of Forster's use of "but Forster, however, writes:

> I have had a university education, you see: and it disposes one to overwork—
>
> that particular conjunction. It is the strength of the academic mind to be fair and see both sides of a question."[45]

Forster's style is unique for it is inclusive of all mode. It varies from the prosaic to the poetic; the ironic, to the romantic; the personal, to the impersonal; the imaginative, to the romantic; the personal, to the impersonal; the imaginative, to the prophetic; the moralistic, to the profound; the classical, to the romantics; the humorous, to the tragic; the sentimental, to the romantic; the humours, to the tragic; the sentimental, to the serious. Herein lies his strength as well as his weakness. Dr. Leavis has pointed out in "The Common Pursuit" that Forster's style is personal.[46] Lard David Cecil, in "Poets and Story-Tellers" writes about Forster's "lyrical sensibility" in the description of nature, the style of the romantic writer is in evidence. Forster loves the earth, Nature, romance, feeling, joys and happiness mingles and blond, and Forster's style acquires beauty and depth.

Forster's notions about a good novel given by him in Aspects of the Novel reveal his ideas in respect of the technique of the novel. According to Forster a great novelist is he, who exquisite in descriptions, tolerant in judgment, ingenious in incidents, vivid in characterization, expert in knowledge, and satisfies all the needs of man's curiosity for the story, human feelings and a sense of values for the characters, intelligence and memory for the plot and "a bar of light" that illumines "the fantastic-prophetically exis,[47] and lastly the aesthetic sense. The good novel continue the stuff of daily life and also the subconscious stuff. Characters in a good novel "have relation to ordinary life", but they expand to embrace "infinity". Forster does not like a novelist who "has a trivial mind and a heavy style"[48] for his work suffers from clumsiness and artificiality, and is marked by lack of emotion and shallowness of judgment. A bad novelist, according to Forster, makes a clumsy device of marriage arid death[49] as a finale. He believes in completion and not expansion in the rounding off, and not in the opening out, of the story. His vision is limited and not extensive. He is unable to bind from within and imposes order from without. He shows us the bony structure and the external form and fails to reach the subterranean spring of vitality. He is unable to stir great chords and fails to produce a resonance in the soul. When he has finished the novel, he does not leave an exhilarating effect. A bad novel lacks unity. It is concerned with the outer life, and does not satisfy the inner life. It is not an imaginative vision of reality and it lacks intrinsic values. A bad novelist in not a master of a perfect technique.

As a novelist, Forster's concern is with the technique of social comedy, of fantasy, of prophecy, of humour, of conversation, of psychological probe, and finally, of style. Forster is "an expert in the dialogue which reveals", a "creator of personalities", a traditionalist who keeps to "the principle of an organic consequential plot"[50] a master of sparkling 'social comedy, and a consummate artist. Forster's technique has been ana lysed by Isherwood in "Lions and Shadows': K. W. Gransden, in E. M. Forster, has pointed out the similarity between Forster and Isherwood in the use of technique. The social comedy of Forster is based on almost the same pattern as employed by Jane Austen in her novels, personal relationship the absence of great scenes of passion, the stress on unimportant happenings, the use of irony and the exposure of pretensions and conceit. But Forster moves from social comedy to fantesy, and from fantasy to prophecy and in the progression from social reality to the prothetic vision. The technique of Forster, too, undergoes change. It is the technique of symbolism, expansion and musical pattern

(B) Characters and Plot

The concern of the English novelists has been with human action determined by motives. The modern novelists are concerned not only with "human experience" but also with "intuitions, visions, and insights."[51] The novelist has direct access to the private life of the individual and he can "descend even deeper and peer into the subconscious"

> He commands all the secret life and he
> must not be robbed of this privilege.[52]

The novelist, according to Forster, may describe the two-dimensional characters who are recognizable because they are constructed round a single idea or quality; he may depict the three-dimensional characters. Modes of characterisation, according to Rene Wellek and Austin Warren in Theory of Literature, are four: "allegoric of quasi-allegoric", "Block", "Static" and "dynamic" or developmental."

In an interview recorded for television by David Jones. Forster confesses that he in not a great novelist for the following reasons:

> "Because I have only got down on to paper
> Really three types of people: the person
> I think I am, the people who irritate me, and
> the people I would like to be."[53]

Forster praises Tolstoy because he "can get hold of all types."[54] where as he is "constricted" in his imagination. Forster is irritated by persons who are hypocritical. He is attracted, on the other hand, by person who are cheerful, independent of mind, tolerant, and endowed with imagination and a sense of humour. In his novels, the characters who resemble Forster are these who are intellectual, liberal, humanistic, and are sceptical of orthodox morality. They are detached, ironical, dispassionate and at the same time have a romantic bent of mind. They have a highly developed sense of beauty, an inward vision and a love of human values. He displays in his novels a horror of the public school that believes in the developed body and the developed mind but not in the developed heart of the rigorous ethical code, that cannot tolerate unconventionality; of the religious orthodoxy, that treads intolerance and encourages fanaticism; of the administrative organization, that relies on efficiency; and, of the bureaucratic attitude, that is always cold and unsympathetic. Forster's antipathy to the enemies of the soul played an important part in the shaping out of his individual vision, coloured by his personal likes and dislikes.

As a novelist, Forster is concerned with the problem of characterization from the outside as well as from the inside. In his novels, there are many types of characters-flat as well as round, conventional as well as unconventional, intellectual as well as intuitive, instinctual as well as intuitive, instinctual as well as redemptive. Forster likes individuals, dislikes social beings, and admires idealists. Forster knows the vices of the English middle-class, which he mentions as charity without love, help without kindness, self-righteousness without tolerance, religious piety without sympathy, remorse without pang of conscience and moral fervour without inner conviction. V.S. Pritchett mentions four types of characters in the novels of Forster—firstly, the faded characters who are efficient due "null" and "dull"; secondly, the Teutonic, who are imaginative but foggy; thirdly, the Latin characters who are course by instinctive; fourthly, the oriental who are "passive but touchy":

"His people swing between two states of

> mind the disinterested and the benighted; disinterested and the benighted.[55]

Swinnerton is of the opinion that Forster can do nothing but vehemently expose conventionality, "caricature it, exaggerate it altogether beyond its natural proportion, punish it, and exalt its opposite which he calls Honesty."[56] The chief conventional characters in the novels of Forster are is, Herriton, Harrit Herriton, Mr. Beebe, Rev. Cuthbert Eager, Cecil Vyse, Herbert Pembroke, Agnes, Mr. Elliott, Mrs. Failling, Henry Wilcox and Ronny Heaslop. Caroline Abbott, Philip Herriton, Charlotte Bartlett, Lucy Honeychurch, and Rickie Elliot get muddled but they recognizes the false nature of conventions and are saved when they break away from conventions. Mrs. Herriton is a true representative of mediocrity and dullness": Harriet Herriton—a Low Church fanatic—is certainly not an agreeable character because of her burly obtuseness and moral blindness. Cecil Vyse fights against Eros and Pallas Athene, against Passion and Truth. He is a cultured man who has a quick eye for interior decoration, and Lucy Honeychurch thinks of him as a man confined in a drawing room without a view. The comic muse does not "disdain the assistance of Mr. Vyse.[57] Cecil Vyse cuts the idea of bringing the Emerson to windy corner and feels happy when he hires one of the unsuitable Flack Villas for the Emersons. Rev. Cuthbert Eager is a high priest of convention. It is he who introduces the medieval theme by describing the life of S. Francis. When Phaethon—"youth all irresponsibility and fire"— succeeds in kissing persephone "tall and slender and pale"[58] Mr. Eager becomes angry. The lovers were ordered to disentangle themselves. Mr. Emerson, on the other hand, pats the Lovers on the backs, and declare that "the lovers must on no account be separated.[59] Lucy Honeychurch hates Mr. Eager because he was a snob and said "unkind things". Mr. Beebe; on the other hand, is kind and considerate from the outside, but a pleasant exterior hides a vulgar mind. He is happy when he learns that Lucy Honeychurch has broken off her engagement with Cecil Vyse.

Angus Wilson, in "A Conversation with E.M. Forster". tells us that Forster does not require any distinguishing marks and external signs to distinguish the goats from the sheep; for when people in the novels of Forster "defend themselves by active means sarcasm, aggressiveness, authoritarianism, and so on, they are usually goats or near-goats".[60] In each novel of Forster there is a significant figure standing outside and constitute, according to E.B.C. Jones, "a touchstone for the participants in the conflict.[61] Mr. Emerson, Stephen Wonham, Mrs. Wilcox and Mrs. Moore stand aloof. Their inner qualities are perceived by the sheep but ignored by the goats. Harriet Herriton is unable to see beauty and goodness in life and her vision is obscured by religious fanaticism. Cecil Vyse is unable to understand passion, for in his outlook there is a scorn of the natural instincts. Mrs. Failing is totally unsympathetic and unimaginative Mr. Emerson, Mrs. Wilcomx, Stephen Wonham, Stewart Ansell, Mrs. More and Godbole have knowledge. The knowledge of Stewart Ansell is based on a powerful intellect, and he makes use of it effectively in the exposure of Agnes Pembroke. Philip Herriton possesses intellect but he is not serious, and therefore, ineffective. The knowledge of Mr. Emerson, Stephen Wonham and Mrs. Elliot is based on their understanding of the power of instincts. In the case of Mrs. Wilcox, Mrs. Moore and Godbole, their knowledge of absolute reality is based on intuition. Agnes Pembroke is conventional, malignant, and her sexual perversion is marked by a love cruelty. She fails to convert Rickie Elliot into a conventional character because she is smashed by steward Ansell and Stephen Wonham. The conventional character like—Mrs. Foiling, Agnes Pembroke, Herbert Pembroke and Honey Wilcox are petrified by conventions. Agnes is "Medusa in Aready" Herbert Pembroke, Forster points out, in to be classed among the goats—the lack of imagination, the business-like brain, the darkness enveloping the soul, the exhaustion of the spiritual life, the concern with material prosperity and success, the unawareness of the intrinsic values, the contempt for knowledge that he possesses are the marks of the "goats" and not of the "sheep":

> "He saw that for all his fine talk about a spiritual life he and but one test for things—for the soul in the life to come. And for this reason humanity, and perhaps such other tribunals as there may be, would assuredly reject him.[62]

Mrs Failing is a character who believes in the majesty of conventions. Henry Wilcox, too, belongs to the category of goats. In the eyes of Margaret Schlegel, he is "criminally muddled."[63] He lacks imagination and is completely unaware of the inner life. Neatness, decision, grit, firmness and steadiness are second-rate virtues and need to be reinforced by love, understanding and sympathy. Henry Wilcox lacks the finer qualities of character and is broken in the end. Ronny Heaslop, too, believes in the conventions of the class to which he belongs. He cannot go against his class an against the people he respects and admire most. He does not want to be pleasant with the Indians because he has something's more important to do—"to dispense justice fearlessly". Forster's use of the unconventional characters is the result of a reaction against materialism in vogue towards the close of the nineteenth century and is a part of, English romanticism's long search for an escape from the respectable, hold out hopes of man's recovery of "strength" and of "love" in modern times.

Feo according to Lionel Trilling in "E.M. Forster—A Study", is the ancestor of Gino Carella, Stephen Wonham and George Emerson. The Perter, in "The Eternal Moment," is the forerunner of the athletic young heroes whose physical beauty and strength redeem their brutality. In Gino Carella and in Stephen Wonham we have a description of the natural man who possesses, "animal vitality" and "rustic strength." Gino is a strange mixture of sweetness and barbarity. He is rude and at times he is no better than a peasant:

> "There was avarice at one moment, and insolence, and politeness, and stupidity, and cunning- and lot us hope that sometime there was love."[64]

The conventional characters are "cold, hardly human" but not so Gino. Gino can be child-like at one moment but the next moment he can be gross;

> "So their talk continued, at one moment full of childishness and tender wisdom, The next moment scandalously gross."[65]

Miss Abbott realises the essential goodness of Gino and she is saved. Stephen Wonham in the instinctual man whose life is in harmony with the earth. His knowledge is perfect since it is based on intuition and not on reason:

> "He had other instincts, but these gave him no trouble. He simply gratified each as it occurred, provided he could do so without grave injury to his Fellow."[66]

Stephen is the natural man:

> "His parents had not for one brief embrace, had found one little interval between the power of the rulers of this world and the power of death. He was the child run in his veins."[67]

He worships Artemis and Demeter – the symbols of fertility, fruition, and continuity. Stephen knows everything about Pan, Nature, and Earth instinctively and his knowledge is divine. The bare room of Stephen has the picture of the Demeter of Cnidus-the goddess who rejoices "in the spring". George Emerson, in "A Room With a View", has a nature that is tender. His father has given him an education which is "free from all the superstition and ignorance that lead men to have one another in the name of God."[68] George Emerson finds happiness in life.

The guardians have a special role to play in the novels of Forster. Their inner qualities are concealed in the beginning but are revealed slowly during the conflict between the forces making for life and the forces destroying life. They are endowed with vision and insight. They fight on the side of goodness and truth and create the necessary moral atmosphere. They are old and can perceive truth. The weak characters perceive their inner qualities. Miss Abbott is dull and amiable but she grows to her full stature in Italy. As a supporter of conventions she goes to Italy to rescue a child:

> "She was here to fight against this place,
> to rescue a little soul who was innocent
> as yet. She was here to champion morality and
> purity, and the holy life of an English home."[69]

Miss. Abbott under goes a great change of heart in Italy. Lilia's love for Gino, the spirit of hilarity prevailing in the opera-house and the shouts of universal joy, the silver stars in the purple sky, violets of a departed spring, Gino's love for the baby and even his physical suffering, all these help Miss Abbott in changing sides and going over to the forces making for life. Placed against "Harriet's burly obtuseness" or "the soulless diplomacy of Mrs. Herriton", Gino appears divine, Miss Abbott is converted and she changes sides, Philip too is saved in the Process:

> "He was content to observe here beauty and
> to profit by the tenderness and
> the wisdom that dwelt within her."[70]

In the end, Miss Abbott reveals to Philip the worth of the true self: Philip has only a glimps of the vision; Miss Abbott is "a goddess to the end", and Philip is raised temporarily to that height and he becomes her worshipper too:

> "To such a height was he lifted, that
> without regret he could now have told
> her that he was her worshipper too".[71]

Mrs. Charlotte Bartlett, in A 'Room With a View', rejects tenderness and becomes peevish. Lucy Honeychurch follows the advice given to her by Miss Bartlett and suppresses her true self and gets muddled:

> "Miss Bartlett, indeed, though not in word, had taught the girl that this our life contains nothing satisfactory. Lucy, though she disliked the teacher, regarded it to her lover".[72]

Miss Bartlett, however, has qualities which she does reveal in the end. She bring Mr. Emerson and Lucy together. Miss Bartlett fights Lucy and George only on the surface but far down in her mind she wants them to be happy. Mr. Emerson is "Charlotte's co-guardian". It is Mr. Emerson who opens the eyes of Lucy and enables her to see her true self. Mr. Emerson, in the end, utterly defeats Mr. Beebe Stewart Ansell is the guardian in 'The Longest Journey,' and he is opposed to Agnes who is conventional. He loves the motives of Agnes and is able to understand her:

> "She wants Rickie, partly to replace another man whom she lost two years ago partly to make something out of him. He is to write in time she will get sick of this. He won't get famous. She will only see how thin he is and how lame. She will long for a Jollier husband, and I don't blame her. And, having made him thoroughly miserable and degraded she will bolt-if and can do it like a lady."[73]

The house Howard end is "a guardian" in itself, though its owner Ruth Wilcox and its house-keeper Miss Avery are also a part of the house and are endowed with intuition and feeling. Mrs. Moore is the guardian, in 'A Passage to India', for she in an intuitive character who is endowed with a " Second sight". It is she who comprehends truth intuitively and it is she who removes the darkness enveloping the soul of Miss Quested. Godbole is the spiritual counterpart of Mrs. Moore who, like Miss Abbott, gains the stature of a goddess. By syllables the invocation of Mrs. Moore are repeated by the crowd after the trial scene, and they become Indianized "Esmiss Esmoor". Ronny Heaslop dislikes the invocation of Mrs. Moore:

> "But he disliked it more than he showed
> it was revolting to hear his mother
> travestied into Esmiss Esmoor, a Hindu goddess."[74]

Forster, in his novels make use of the redemptive characters Mr. Emerson is a redemptive character because he save Lucy Honeychurch from unhappiness. Another redemptive character is Mr. Failing in "The Longest Journey". He, too, is a saviour, Mr. Failing has not a practical mind but he is kind. His voice is the voice of protest against the materialism of the moneyed class. The redemptive characters like Miss Abbott, Mr. Emerson, Ruth Wilcox, Ansell and Mrs. Moore Philip Herriton, Lucy Honeychurch, Margaret, Rickie and Miss Quested respectively. Ruth Wilcox and Mrs. Moore are Characters who have something of the forces of life, the kindness of Mr. Failing, the instinctive life of Stephen Wonham, the goodness of Mr. Emerson, and the unattainable vision of Miss Abbott who, in the eyes of Philip, is "A Superior being—a goddess". Ruth Wilcox, of Quaker stock, has a sense of mystery and is in touch with the unseen life. She is endowed with inward Light. Her tenderness, her gentleness, her intuitive faculty and her power of comprehension make her the very embodiment of the Feminine Spirit. She nourishes the life of the Spirit and knows Life Instinctively. She is not intellectual, nor even alert, but nevertheless, she gives the "idea of greatness" :

> "Margaret, zig-zagging with her friends over
> thought and art, was conscious of a personality

> that transcended their own and dwarfed their activities.
> there was no bitterness in
> Mrs. Wilcox; there was not oven criticism; She was loveable, and no ungracious or uncharitable word had passed her lips.[75]

She does not care for the outer life of material prosperity but dossier for "inward light"; in fact, the tenderness, the innocence, the insight, the instinctive kindness and the innate goodness of Ruth Wilcox make her a lovable character:

> She came of Quaker stock, and he and his family, formerly Dissenters, were now members of the Church of England.

"The rector's sermons had at for 'a more inward light', adding, 'not so much for myself as for baby' (Charles). Inward light must have been granted, for he heard no complaints in later years."[76]

Mrs. Moore is another redemptive character who develops to her full stature when she is ready to receive a new vision of life in the caves. She is cut-off from all external action and undergoes a psychic experience. She realises the futility of religion, of family ties, of marriage and of all personal relationships. She is a real character; Aziz meets her:

> "Advancing, her found that she was old. A fabric bigger than the mosque fell to pieces, and he did not know whether he was glad or sorry. She was older than Hamidullah Begum, with a red face and white hair. Her voice had deceived him."[77]

It is India that reveals to her a reality deeper than any reality experienced by her in the West. It is older than Christianity, older than the creation of the world-"the undying worm itself". "A Passage to India" is conceived according to "Values much better apprehended by Mrs. Moore".

The major characters of the novels of Forster are the male Protagonists-Philip Herriton, Cyril Fielding and Rickie Elliot.

Philip is an intellectual snob who stands at a distance from humanity. He is an observer who passes through the world without colliding with it. He is purged of evil by suffering. Gino tortures Philip and this Proves to be his individual salvation. He gains his humanity and learns to love. The tender core of his heart responds to life and Philip is saved. Miss Abbott sympathizes with the lot of Philip who is deinied fulfillment. She says to Philip:

> "Oh, you appreciate me! She burst out again.
> I wish you didn't. You appreciate us all.
> See good in all of us. And all the time you
> are dead-dead-dead, look, why aren't your angry?[78]

She further says:

> "You are so splendid, Mr. Herriton, that I can't bear to see you wasted. I can't bear, she has not been good to your mother".[79]

The word 'dead' repeated thrice emphasizes the sterility of intellect. D. H. Lawrence, too disliked Bertrand Russell, J.M. Keynes, and Duncan Grant:

> He hated them all with a passionate hatred
> And said they were "dead, dead, dead."[80]

Rickie Elliot is taken in by conventions. Agnes, who is only "the semblance of reality" is real to Rickie for his ideas distort the real character of Agnes and of Gerald. Rickie becomes the victim of his diseased imagination: "He loved, he was loved, he had seen death and other things: but the heart of all things was hidden."[81] It is Ansell who tries to save Rickie by rescuing him from the clutches of Agnes and by disclosing him the truth about Mrs. Elliot and Robert.

The Masculine Spirit reveal itself in action. Henry Wilcox is an example of the Masculine Spirit. He relies not on

Imagination and the love of the earth but on work, the sense of duty, grit and determination. He lacks insight, sympathy, and feeling but possesses the business acumen and the possessive instinct. Paul Wilcox and Charles Wilcox, like Henry Wilcox, are materialists and they have no idea of personal relationships of private life, of music and my story and passion. They treat life, marriage, deatn and social revealed in characters who are gentle, imaginative and sympathetic. Ruth Wilcox is the embodiment of the Feminine Spirit. Her Innate goodness makes her a loveable character:

> "Her tenderness; Her innocence: The wonderful innocence that was hers by the Gift of God. Ruth know no more of Worldly wickedness and wisdom than did the flowers in her garden, or the grass in her field".[82]

Margaret Schlegel and Helen Schlegel are dedicated to the inner life. Margaret does not believe in the medieval outlook. She wants to connect the outer life with the life of the spirit. Helen is attractive and impulsive and wants to reach the inner life through the body.

The success of a novel depends on the skill of the novelist to construct a well-knit consequential plot, and on his creative ability to make up a scene and create living character. The characters in the novels of Forster, excluding the conventional characters, do change and develop when they come into contact with new experience. The portraits of Henry Wilcox, Cecil Vyse, Mrs. Wilcox and of some other characters are firmly and deftly drawn by Forster, Henry Wilcox's portrait is firmly drawn. Henry Wilcox has all the characteristics of the rugged individual who succeeds in life because he is efficient, firm and determined. Forster has described: the face, not square as his son's; the chin, firm in outline; the lips, curtained by a moustache: the eyes, unflinching and steady; and, finally, the forehead:

> "The forehead, too, was life Charles's. High and Straight, brown and polished, merging abruptly into temples and skull, it had the effect of a bastion that protected his head from the world. At times it had the effect of a blank wall. He had dwelt behind it, Intact and happy, for fifty years."[83]

The Portrait of Cecil Vyse is adequate a Gothic statue;

> "Tall and refined, with shoulders that seemed braced square by an effort of the will, and a head that was tilted a little higher than the usual level of vision, he resembled these fastidious cathedral."[84]

Forster's reaction against conventions produces his best satire. It is because of his comic vision that some of the characters Mrs. Herriton, Herbert Pembroke, Harriet, Charlotte are turned into caricatures; in his treatment of the Anglo-Indians in 'A Passage to India' we are "still too close to caricature and melodrama", Evie is portrayed ironically by Forster. She is handsome, dark-eyed, firm-lipped, and built strongly. She too, is close to caricature. Ronny Heaslop, too, is portrayed in the same vein, we hear "the self -satisfied lift" of his words and see "the mouth moving so complacently and competently beneath the little rod nose".[85] Jackey, in Howards End, is too close to melodrama whether the portraits are real of "close to caricature", they are clear, well- defined and unforgettable. Even the portrait of Ruth Wilcox is firmly drawn we remember the tall figure, the beautiful head, and the trailing dross of Ruth Wilcox:

> She approached Just as Helen's letter had described her, trailing noiselessly over the lawn, and there was actually a wisp of hay in her hands"[86]

The characters, in the novels of Forster, have been cast in certain moulds so as to fall in a general pattern, and they express the inmost beliefs and ideas of the novelist. They are the outcome of his individual outlook and insight. The best characters of Forster are a projection of the qualities of Forster, his goodness and kindness, his genuine understanding and friendship, his modesty and quietism, his donnish whimsy. Forster's strange mixture of qualities has monitored by Stephen Spender in world within world.

Angus Wilson is critical of Forster's "saints" and "damned". Forster's ethics influenced enormously Angus Wilson: "Indeed a great deal of what I have written has been an attempt to soften the rigorous of what I feel to be his Calvinism, perhaps by knocking some of his saints on the head and by liberating some of his damned."[87] Angus Wilson agrees with Forster's idea that "human virtue and salvation are not a matter of works but an expression of an inner grace".[88] Forster's "weaknesses are personal ones", according to Dr. Leavis, Forster's unconventional characters possess the solid qualities of the natural instincts and the generous impulses of the natural instincts.

The conventional characters lack depth and vitality but for the purpose of satire they are good enough we admire the characters who are cheerful, tolerant, sympathetic and imaginative but when admiration has been fully expressed, the feeling returns that the characters are caged in the author's mind, unable to escape in "actuality", Forster has mentioned, in 'The Paris Review' Interviews, the models from which some characters in his novels have been drawn. Forster concludes:

> When all goes well, the original material soon disappears, and a character who belongs to the book and nowhere also emerges.[89]

Forster thinks highly for plot. In Aspect of the Novel, he distinguishes between the plot and the story:

> "We have defined the story as a narrative of events arranged in there time sequence. A plot is also a narrative of events, the emphasis falling oh causality. 'The king died and then the queen died', is a story, 'the king died and queen died in grief' is a plot.[90]

In this way Forster constitute that plot is more important than the story, because story tells only events but the plot deals the whole situation, the condition, the setting and the atmosphere of the scenery. He himself is such an excellent story teller. It is true that his artistry is at a highest in those of his plot. Which contain many carefully laid clause which may be picked up later in the novel's development. This is one reason why reading Forster's Novels can be so rewarding. The subtlety office plot structure some time escapes a first reading. There are rarely any uncountable loose ends. In other words where a character is not essential in the story for the development of the plot, he can be rapidly dispatched. In his most outstanding novels Howards End and A Passage to India, the sudden death of Mrs. Wilcox and Mrs. Moore came in the notice of the readers but these ladies exert their influence on the plot long after their demise.

In other words we can say that plot is narrative of events based on the logic of cause and the effect while the story is merely a narrative of events. Forster does not except the conventional definition of plot in which emphasis is given on cause effect theory; He wants that plot should be as flexible as life. The plot should not be contrived by sacrificing human qualities. His concept of plot is that:

> "The plot instead of finding human being more or less out to its requirements, as they are in the drama finds than enormous, shadowy and intractable and three quarters hidden like an ice burg".

References

1. Robert C. Rathbern : The Makers of the British Novels, From Jane Austen toJoseph Conrad, (Univ. of Minnesota Press, 1958), p. 22.

2. Edith, C. Batch and Bonamy Dobree : The Victorians and After, (London, 1950), pp. 75-6.
3. Wright Morris: The Living Novel — A Symposium (New York, 1957), p. 122.
4. *Ibid.,* p. 121.
5. Routh R.V. English Literature and Ideas (London, 1950) p. 2.
6. Woolf Virgina the Novel of E.M. Forster (London, 1947), p. 106.
7. Scott - Games, R.A.: The Making of Literature (London, 1956), p. 237.
8. Fox Ralph: The Novel and The People (Moscow, 1956), p. 70.
9. Van Chant, Dorothy: The English Novel (New York, 1961), p. 8.
10. Mondilo, A.A.: Time and The Novel (London, 1952), p. 235.
11. Aspect of the Novel, p. 24.
12. Savage, D.S.: The Withred Branch,(London, 1950), p. 12.
13. Booth, C.Wayne: The Rhetoric of Fiction (Chicago, 1961), p. 395.
14. Drew Elizabath: The Novel (New York 1963), p. 22.
15. Cowley Malcolm: The Writers at Works (London, 1962), p. 26.
16. *Ibid.,* p. 26
17. *Ibid.,* p. 26-27.
18. Where Angels Fear to Tread, p. 121.
19. A Passege to India, p. 257.
20. Aspect of The Novel, p. .40.
21. McConkey, James: The Novels of E.M. Forster (Ithaca, New York, 1957), p. 21.
22. Auerbach Erich: Mimesis (Princeton Univ. Press, 1953), p. 121.
23. Cox C.B.The Free Spirit (Oxford Univ. Press, 1963), p. 57.
24. Green, F.C.: The Mind of Proust (Cambridge, 1949), p. 521.
25. *Ibid.,* p. 18.

26. Kettle, Arnold: An Introduction to The English Novel (London, 1951), p. 126.
27. Where Angels Fear to Tread, p. 150.
28. Cowley, Malcolm: Writers at Work (London, 1962), p. 29.
29. Aspect of the Novels, p. 153.
30. Two Cheers for Democracy, p. 117.
31. Aspect of the Novels, p. 155.
32. Where Angels Fear to Tread, p. 104.
33. A Room with a View, p. 34.
34. *Ibid.*, p. 35.
35. *Ibid.*, p. 45.
36. *Ibid.*, p. 215.
37. Aspect of the Novels, p. 154.
38. Howard End, p. 33.
39. A Passage to India, p. 78.
40. *Ibid.*, p. 79.
41. A Passage to India, p. 280.
42. J.B. Beer: The Achievement of E.M. Forster (London, 1962), p. 207.
43. H.J. Oliver: The Art of E.M. Forster (Malbourne University Press, 1960), p. 35.
44. Lionel Trilling: E.M. Forster — A Study (London, 1944), p. 32.
45. Two Cheers for Democracy, The Raison d, Etro of Criticism in the Arts, p. 130.
46. F.R. Leavis : "E.M. Forster, The Common Pursuit, 1952 (A Penguine Book, 1962), p. 275.
47. Aspects of the Novel, p. 101.
48. *Ibid.*, p. 32.
49. Two Cheers for Democracy, The Raison d' Etre of Criticism in the Arts, p. 129.
50. H.V. Raouth : English Literature and Ideas in the Twentieth Century (London, 1946), p. 62.
51. Robert Humphery: Stream of Consciousness in the Modern

Novel, 1954 (University of California Press, Third Printing, 1958), p. 7.

52. Aspects of the Novel, p. 81.
53. David Jones: E.M. Forster on his Life and his Books, An Interview Recorded for Television (The Listener January 1, 1959, Vol. LXI, No. 1533), p. 11.
54. *Ibid.*, p. 11.
55. V.S. Pritchett: Mr. Forster's New Year, New Statesman, Saturday, 27th December, 1958, Vol. LVI, No. 1450, p. 912.
56. Frank Swinnerton : The Geavgian Literary Scene (Everyman's Library, No. 943, London, 1938), p. 290.
57. A Room with a View, p. 126.
58. *Ibid.*, p. 65.
59. *Ibid.*, p. 69.
60. Angus Wilson, A Conversation with E.M. Forster, Encounter, Vol. IX, No. 5, November, 1957, p. 55.
61. E.B.C. Jones: E.M. Foster and Virginia Woolf, The English Novelists, Edited by Derek Verschoyle (London, 1936), p. 273.
62. The Longest Journey, p. 188.
63. Howards End, p. 287.
64. K.W. Gransden : E.M. Forster (London, 1962), p. 11.
65. Where Angels Fear to Tread, p. 35.
66. *Ibid.*, p. 47.
67. The Longest Journey, p. 268.
68. *Ibid.*, p. 269.
69. A Room with a View, p. 31.
70. Where Angels Fear to Tread, p. 108.
71. *Ibid.*, p. 129.
72. *Ibid.*, p. 160.
73. A Room with a View, p. 143.
74. The Longest Journey, p. 94.
75. A Passage to India, p. 219.
76. Howards End, p. 73.

77. *Ibid.*, p. 85.
78. A Passage to India, p. 22.
79. Where Angels Fear to Tread, p. 131.
80. *Ibid.*, p. 131.
81. Bertrand Russell, Portraits from Memory and Other Essays (London, 1956), p. 104.
82. The Longest Journey, p. 166.
83. Howards End, p. 85.
84. *Ibid*, p. 86.
85. A Room with a View, p. 93.
86. A Passage to India, p. 50.
87. Howards End, p. 22.
88. Angus Wilson: "A Conversation with E.M. Forester" Forster, Encounter, Vol. IX, No. 5, November, 1957, p. 53.
89. *Ibid.*, p. 53.
90. Malcolm Cowley, Writers at work, The Paris Review, Interviews Edited by Malcolm Cowley, Interviewers P.N. Furbank and F.J.H. Haskell (Mercury Books No.29, London, 1962), pp. 30-1.

7

Conclusion

Forster is a critic as well as a creative artist. He calls his fiction 'the mixed art' of criticism and creation. His novels show the critical and creative states of his mind. As a critic of society he writes the comedy and social satire and exposes the purblind morality, prim formality and the hypocritical piety of the English middle-class. As a creative writer, he writes fantasy and prophesy and explores self. As writer of fiction, he is deeply committed to the claims of human being. He is interested in the individual who lives a free, independent and distinct life in his own, as opposed to the social being who adheres to convention. The novel in the hand of Forster, exists not only to observe and criticise social life but also to create what is true, beautiful and significant in human life.

The novels of Forster are in part a criticism of the conventions of the English middle-class, and in part they are an emphatic assertion of the claims of the heart against the intellectual arrogance of the modern age. They are shaped by the new trends in the modern thought and are at the same time a continuation of the long tradition of the English liberal humanism of intellectual curiosity and critical intelligence of good will and trust, of tolerance and justice, of individual freedom and respect for others. Forster knows the power of free spirit. His mystic faith in the individual, his non-political liberalism, his dislike of authority, and his belief in individual freedom, are his "attitudes". He rejected 'Laissez Faire' economics but showed his preference for 'Laissez Faire' "in the world of spirit"[1] faced with the incapable dilemma of his age. Forster, however, preserves an open mind and is not prepared to forgo the basic liberal principle of freedom. His fiction has brought fruition his conviction in the worth of the individual and in the inner strength and freedom of the human spirit. Rickie Elliot's club foot perhaps symbolizes "an inherited weakness in his liberal idealism".[2]

The liberals of the pre war period believed that reason, education, kindness, goodwill and trust, could control evil and bring about understanding among the people but they were not sufficiently aware of "the limit of human nature and the power of evil"[3] and so their faith in progress, when first World War broke out "ended necessarily in despair. "Order, unity and harmony could not be achieved through reason. Forster's 'agonistic mind' undermeans his liberal humanistic value in 'A Passage to India.' The echo in the Marabar Caves destroys all values: "everything exists, nothing has value".[4] Forster however does not lose contact with his true self. He has preserved his faith in the freedom of the human spirit. Forster does not make a categorical statement of the nature of reality, and man's position in the universe. He, however has tried to indicate in 'A Passage to India' "the human predicament in the universe which is not so far comprehensible to our mind"[5] The outlook of the Victorian philosophers was "partly philosophical and partly moral".[6] The outlook of Forster on the other hand is partly philosophical and partly imaginative. The creative artist in literature, according to Robert Liddell, is not always "a person of the highest intelligence for his mind is imaginative rather than philosophical".[7]

Forster is a creative artist who is imaginative and philosophical. It is his philosophic mind which enables him to see truth clearly. It is his imaginative mind which enables him to see truth intuitively. Forster's attitude towards life are based on the diverse aspect of his complex mind liberalism, individualism, agnosticism. According to Dr. Arnold Kettle they are useful terms insofar as they refer to his attitudes. Forster distrusts labels and categories and uses terms in a general way; it is, therefore, not surprising to learn that his "novels are conceived in terms of moral generalization".[8] His point of view is the spontaneous expression of his vision of reality, of his love of humanity, of his inmost beliefs and ideas, of his inner conviction and of his imaginative comprehension of life. Forster attaches his values to personal relations, private affection, voyage for spirituality, to friendship and love, to sincerity and good will to leisure and pleasure, and to the English countryside and its traditional way of life. He likes people who are cheerful, courageous and broad minded. He likes gaiety and earnestness of purpose but not seriousness which makes life dreary and unhelpful. In an interview recorded for television by David Jones, Forster said about himself:

> "But if I have had any influence I should be very glad that I had induced people to enjoy this wonderful world in to which we are born, and of course to help others to enjoy it too."[9]

Forster again tells us, that his absence of religious views "developed rather slowly", but since the age of 24, I have had more or less the same attitude:

> "What I do see more clearly because reason can't solve everything, but I want it to solve as many things as it can. Also I am more conscious of my own smallness and the smallness of this planet; but I don't find this bothers me much, do you?"[10]

Forster is aware of the limitations of the human knowledge: "We can't under stand each other, except in a rough and ready way; we can't reveal our selves, even when we want to; what we call intimacy is only a make shift; perfect knowledge is an illusion."[11]

Forster however makes a statement of his philosophy towards life. "The universe is so fantastic and uncertain that I find, I am very thankful for having I don't feel any remorse about it. All my comforts may be taken away at any moment, but while they last I am delighted to enjoy them".[12]

Aley Hasan is a writer about the double attitude of Forster in respect of the nuclear war and the global mass: "I have once or twice spoken on the subject of the nuclear business in Cambridge, but I am very pessimistic. At the same time I am hopefull. I have got that double attitude as I think so many of us do have."[13]

Forster believes that both humble people and well-informed people have got this double attitude, and this explains, perhaps, the presentation of his novels of the opposing attitudes of pessimism and idealism, of mysticism and scepticism, and of paganism and moral belief. In spite of Forster's philosophy, the vision of Forster seems to be directed to the basic themes of his novels. It is the theme of truth, of personal relationship, of private life, of inner conflict, it is the theme of reality, metaphysical concepts, it is the theme of appearance and reality of society and individual. Freedom for the individual in the fixed class structure is the vision of Forster, lies in self-awareness, the unfolding of the inner potentialities for good, "in the fulfillment of the inner urges and in the attainment of a balanced life of just proportion and inner stability, and also, in the true understanding of the nature good and evil. In the bourgeois society, the social being of man is sundered from its living center: contact between the two can be established only by an act of imagination. The success of the novels of Forster depend upon his imaginative understanding of the human life. Truth is the moral focus of all his novels and it gives unity and meaning to life. Forster if constantly haunted by the idea of permanence in the midst of the constant flux and flow. It is the hard core of self that can withstands the pressure of the conventional morality. The spring of morality and joy lie within. He, therefore wants the individual to the participated in the eternal life. "The Sunday Statement" in its Editorial writes: "The writer engaged in a work of fiction that may give joy to millions and than prove of enduring value is not a traitor."[14]

It is the recognition of the soul or truth that gives an enduring value to the novels of Forster.

Forster is faced with the problem of finding in fiction a significant form which can express his inner conviction and limit, the subject-matter of his novels to his particular point of view. Thematic form gives to his novels a firmness of structure and a complex pattern. The authors voice adds something to the story I 'accent' or 'value'. The author at the mid-point is the mediator; it is not at the poles of the real and the ideal but at the center that he gains, the correct perspective. From the exalted point of view, Forster enables us to see that the physical reality is incomplete without the spiritual reality. From the mid-point of view, he enables us to discern the boundary of human suffering and sorrow, and also the beauty and mystery of the unknown reality. The mid=point of view, therefore, involves a double attitude, detachment and attachment, aloofness from the human tangle and compassion for suffering humanity.

Life, to Forster is an integrated image of the body and the soul. Perfection and imperfection, good and evil, the flesh and the spirit, are infect inseparable. The soul is real and Forster's stress is on the inner life. It is the recognition of soul, that gives enduring value to life. The soul the hard core in men, alone can resist evil. It contains the opposing principle and provides plot; it conceals it self by creating illusions and provide the subject-matter of society and self; it provide the theme of personal relationships; it imposes order on the raw material of life; it creates the two opposing way of life; and it provides the most significant clue to the reality of man and to that of the universe. Thus, the creative work of Forster is in part a reaction against materialism and intellectual arrogance and in part an assertion of the life of the spirit. His novels are the true expression of his philosophy of life. Forster knows how to combine his way of thinking and reality in an integrated work of art. It is one of the outstanding traits of Forster's complex mind that he is able to fuse the divers parts of human experience in to an organic hole. Forster's stress is on such values as the lucidity of the whole, the clarity of the individual philosophy, the worklessness of the worldly life, the importance of the inner life, the cultivation of the true being, the liberation of the personality from the darkness of illusion, and the realization of the true self through love. Herbert Gold writes about the mystery of life:

> "That is, life has meaning as the shadows of Plato's cave have meaning—as flickering glimpses through fire of something beyond life, some thing perfect and unchanging and finally unknowable by men."[15]

Forster in 'A Passage to India' writes: "Not for them was an infinite goal behind the stars, and they never sought it. But wastefulness descended on them now, as on other occasions; the shallow of the shadow of a dream fell over there clear out interest, and object never seen again seemed messages from another world."[16]

The inner life is timeless and space less. It gives a clue to the eternal life and it gives satisfaction which can never be obtained from the outer life. Edwin Muir rightly says:

> "Seen against eternity the life of man is complete story, seen against time it is an unfinished one, a part of endless change, a fleeting picture on an unstable substance."[17]

The inner life is an oasis in the desert of social relationship. The failure of achieving harmony within results is panic and emptiness. The inner life gives enduring joy because it is a perfect world. Bertrand Russell writes:

> "Until I was about forty, I should think, I got the sort of satisfaction that Plato says that you can get out of mathematics. It was an eternal world, it was a timeless world, It was a world where there was a possibility of certain kind of perfection, and I

> certainly got something analogous to religious satisfaction out of it."[18]

Personal relationship forms the hard core of Forster's philosophy of life. In his personal relationships, the individual's tenderness comes in the individual needs company, love and warmth of affection. About the personal relationshipt of Aziz and Fielding, Glenn O' Allen remarks:

> "And then, as the word ends fielding and Aziz, who's friendship had been reborn the tank at man, are preserved from consummate union as the hundred voices of the earth speaks out and say, "No, not yet" (not in time) and the sky says No, not here (not in space)".[19]

A close study of Forster's novels reveals Forster's notions about human suffering. In "Where Angels Fear to Tread" the eyes of Miss Abbott are full of infinite pity and discern the boundaries of sorrow, "Her hands were folded round the sufferer stoking him gentle, for even a goddess can do no more than that".[20] Suffering purges the soul of Philip Harriton and he is saved. Mr. Emerson asks Lucy Honeychurch to marry George Emerson in.......A Room With a View', Lucy is Frightened:

> "You have frightened me, she moaned. Everything she fell sobbing into the chair. I am caught in the tangle. I must suffer and grow old away from him. I can't break the whole of life for his sake. They trusted me".[21]

Mrs. Elliot in 'The Longest Journey' suffers when Stephen Wonham is born. She begins to love Rickie Elliot, and a curious thing happened. Her second child drew her towards her first. She begins to love Rickie also, and to be more than useful to him. And as she revived, so did her capacity for suffering. Life more important grew better.

And Helan Dimb with fright, but trying to keep calm for the child's lake, and Miss Avery, calm but murmuring tenderly, "No oneever told that he will have a child. They also reminded her that horror is not the end. To what ultimate harmony we tend, she did not know, but there seemed great chance that a child would be born in to the world to take the great chances of beauty and adventure that the world offers."[22] Beauty emanates from suffering. Hope emanates from death. Through sorrow thesoul is purged of evil. Sorrow is, therefore, a source of joy. 'To Leonard, intent to his private sin, there come the conviction of innate goodness elsewhere'.

"Again and again must the drum, the tape, the goblins stalk over the universe before joy can be purged of the superficial. Is war rather paradoxical and arose from his sorrow? "Death destroys a man, the idea of death saves him." That is the best account of it that has yet been given. Squalor a tragedy can beckon to all that great in us, and strengthen the wings of love".[23]

Hamidullah in 'A Passage To India' can't feel the sense of sorrow at the death of Mrs. Moore and if for a moment- the sense of communion in sorrow comes, it passes.

"How, indeed, is it possible for one human being to be sorry for all the sadness that meets him on face of the earth, for the pain that is endured, not only by men, but by animals, and plants, and perhaps by the stone."[24]

All life according to Buddha is suffering. He, therefore advocates a complete renunciation of life. The Buddha's compassion is "of the understanding rather than the direct sympathy of the heart which carries within it, the impulse to help".[25] Forster's compassion for suffering humanity is the result of his direct sympathy. He is friendly, kind, sympathetic and loving towards week characters who suffer and endure life. His philosophy is the spontaneous expression of his love for mankind. The springs of vitality and sensibilities lie with in the individual and he explores them. Forster feels sincerely and strongly, and he expresses his convictions with simplicity, candour and courage. He believes strongly that the source of joy and perennial happiness is within the world can be saved from destruction by means of kindness, tenderness, sympathy and compassion. While reading his novels we are aware of the writer whose vision emanates from the inward core of his "complex"[26] personality. Linked with the Forster's idea of human sufferings, is the idea of fate. It is interesting to study Forster's concept of fate. He is aware of forces external as well as internal—that determine the course of events. In 'Where Angels Fear to Tread' the death of Gino's haby is attributed to fate; it is the result of Harriet's crime, the negligence of perfetta, the diplomacy of Mrs. Harriten, and the weakness of Philip Harriten. Everyone, infact, contributes to the tragedy. George Emerson believes that is pure co-incidence that they together: It is I have reflected. It is fate. Everythings fate. We are flung together by fate, drawn apart by fate, flung together drawn apart. The twelve winds blow us, we settle nothing. Aziz in 'A Passage to India' talks about fate when he is arrested and is set free when Miss Quested withdraw the charge:

> "It is fate, he said and it is fate, when he was imprisoned in Mohurrum. All that existed, in that terrible time, was affection, and affection was all that he felt in the first painful moment of his freedom."[27]

Godbole explains 'that nothing can be performed by isolation'. The evil action is performed by everyone—by Aziz, by the guide, by Godbole and by Fielding:

> "I am informed that the evil action was performed in the Marabar Hills, and that highly esteemed English lady is now seriously ill in consequence. My answer to that is this: that action is performed by Dr. Aziz. He is stopped and sucked in his then cheeks. The guide performed it. He stopped again. You performed it. Now he had an air of daring and of coyness. It was performed by me."[28]

Forster holds a unique place in history of the English novel. As a writer of fiction, he is a link between the old tradition of the English novel and the new trends in modern fiction. Forster is a traditionalist who regards the story, the plot, the characters and the social scene as essential aspects of the novel. His philosophy, however, is characteristic of the Modern Age. Forster is a modern novelist for he regards the theme as more important than the subject-matter; the aesthetic form, as more significant than the structure; the easy rhythm, as more convincing than the rigid pattern; the life by values, as more enduring than the life in time; the shifting point of view, as more reliable than the fixed point of view; and symbolism, as a better instrument than realism in the proper understanding of life.

The novels of Forster are the product of his humanistic philosophy. His philosophy is shaped by his bourgeois upbringing, his personal experiences, and his travels. His bourgeois upbringing has given him "a middle-class slant" upon life; his individualism has given him his faith in the individual and his belief in personal relationships. His sad experience at Tonbridge School developed his dislike of the public-school system. Cambridge, on the other hand, stands for sweet reasonableness. The architecture of King's College becomes the symbol of his own view of life, life is a mystery as well as a muddle. The study of the Classics has given him the Greek view of life—the division of man into the rational part and the animal part, the absence of the Christian concept of Free Will, the stole notion of learning by suffering, the strain of pessimism and of settled gloom, and the passion for truth and beauty. His experience of the Mediterranean world has given him the pagan outlook as opposed to the medieval outlook. The sweet reasonableness of Cambridge, the paganism of the Mediterranean, world, the hoary past of Egypt and Alexandria, and the spiritualism of India have contributed to the development of his philosophy and helped him in understanding the meaning of life. Forster attaches great importance to aesthetic emotions, personal relationships, sincerity, individual freedom, likes for spirituality tolerance, and diversity. The paganism and the aesthetic approach of Forster are a necessary corrective to his bourgeois outlook. His outlook, therefore, is an expression of his philosophical reaction against crass materialism of the urban civilization. The philosophy Forster is the focus of his novels. It enables him to select the subject-matter of his novels. It gives to his novels an artistic unity. His philosophic vision enables him to observe and criticize social life; his moral vision enables him to judge and to classify human beings into moral categories; and his creative act makes him blend the diverse elements into an organic whole. Forster's vision is double since he is aware of the two ways of life—the civilized and the pagan, the cultivated and the wild, the rational and the imaginative. The action of his novels is based upon the interaction of the opposing points. His philosophy actually directs his vision to maintain a significant view. His vision includes the common place and the outlook for his novels extraordinary, the pleasant and the unpleasant, the beautiful and the repulsive. The union of the opposite tendencies is possible only in a state of high concentration. In the novels of Forster there is an integration of the opposite tendencies, muddle and mystery, nightmare and vision, squalor and splendor, comedy and tragedy, light and darkness. Forster has worked out the contrast between the two opposing modes of life into diverse fictional forms, elaborate social comedy, fantasy and prophecy. Forster's double vision has developed the theme of his novels. His pagan outlook is revealed in 'Where Angels Fear to Tread'; his personal dilemmas in 'The Longest Journey'; his integrated vision in 'Howards End'; and his prophetic vision in 'A Passage to India'. Forster in his novels, deals with life realistically as well as imaginatively. Goldsworthy Lowes Dickinson has pointed out that Forster's constant preoccupation in his novels is "to bring realistic life into contact with the background of values".[29] Neither losing touch with reality nor missing contact with the inner spirit of man, Forster has succeeded in achieving a "singleness of vision" in 'A Passage to India' Oliver W. Larkin says:

> The integration of art presupposes a
>   personal integration in the artist,
> as lively a curiosity about others
>   as about himself, and a willingness

> to surrender a degree of his mental
> and aesthetic autonomy.[30]

If Forster, after having struggled against his own inner tensions and moral dilemmas, seems to have achieved harmony in 'A Passage to India', for every disturbing element has been properly controlled and contributes to the integrated whole. It is in India that by some grace of God, according to Morton Dauwen Zabel, Forster is "permitted a sight of that farther goal of the human spirit which lies beyond the rational and aggressive principles of western life".[31] Forster's outlook is inclusive and not exclusive; it embraces life's dichotomy and creates a true and living image of life which is a fusion of the contrary principles good and evil. His philosophy is focussed on the totality of being and gives us a sense of communion with something beyond the visible frame of the conventional bourgeois society.

The vision of the novelist is social when he studies the life of man in society; his vision is private, when he studies the life of man centered in the spiritual reality. The novel, according to Mark Schorer, exists at a point of intersection of society and self. The poles of "novelistic tension" are society and self, good and evil, appearance and reality. Forster is the novelist of criticism and sensibility, philosophy and act, since he brings society and self-together in a durable antithesis. His novels deal with the evil of conventions as well as with the glorious visions entertained by the true self. Thus fiction exists for him not only to criticize and protest but also to immortalize what it creates. By bringing together society and self in juxtaposition Forster is able to bring out the contrast between the false and the true. His outer vision exposes pretentiousness and evils of society, whereas his inner vision explores the splendor of self. Thus he is the observer of the exterior and the guardian of the interior. Forster is interested in the individual experience, which is real, true and significant. He has, however, a mystic faith in the individual. In his novels there is neither the "rigorous view" nor the laxity of the "permissive view". His novels are a plea for natural life as opposed to the conventional life of the English middle-class. Forster is an Edwardian novelist who, like George Meredith, protests against the materialism of his times. He is more concerned with the inner life than the outer life" and he is "all for acceptance of 'life', bare and naked, with all its instinctive richness and emotional fervour". Forster' vigorous protest, like the protest of the Victorian writers, is "against materialism and complacency, against aesthetic and moral blindness". Forster is a classicist because the romantic intention is the exploration of the soul. By taking up the subject of society and self, Forster deals with the intersection of two types of characters, the conventional and the unconventional; and with two types of society, the Great Society and the Little Society; and with the two kinds of life – the Good and the Bad. Forster's genius lies in his attempt to blend 'the social vision with the poetic vision of life. The novels of Forster are, therefore, a criticism of the English middle-class and its conventions, and also a plea for the development of the inner life. Irony is the moral focus of his novels; it is the point of illumination at the. intersection of Seeming and Being. The moral philosophy of Forster is his dominant idea of truth which he calls by different names – soul, self, inner life, personal relationships. His act and vision, which he calls the writer's "sensitiveness" or the creative impulse, enables him to select the raw material, process it by means of technique, and impose a significant form upon it by an act of creation. Forster has been able to find a form, which expresses neatly and clearly the view of reality held by him. His point of view gives to the subject-matter of his novels a formalized neatness, an intellectual solidity, an emotional exuberance, and a unity of feeling. Forster has discovered a new technique simple, firm, and solid structure based on an antithetical plot and a complex pattern evolved out of symbol and meaning, through the use of a moral focus. The novel turns in the fiction of the Twentieth Century – the fiction of, among others, Virginia. The Edwardian novelists -- H.G. Wells, John Galsworthy, and Arnold Bennett – wrote of unimportant things and made "The trivial and the transitory appear the true and the enduring".[32] All art, according to Leon Edel, is "an attempt to achieve an artistic vision of experience and of beauty and a constant search for truth".[33] E.M. Forster, too by the help of his philosophy has attempted to achieve beauty and truth in his novels and has enriched English fiction. His realism curbs his vision, his classicism restrains his romanticism his philosophical creativity, explains his different recurring themes, and his high moral seriousness controls his paganism. His novels ill retain their original freshness and charm. 'A Passage to India' still retains its popularity. Santha Rama Rau dramatized it. Frank Hauser staged it at Oxford in January 1959; from Oxford it went to the Comedy Theatre in London and on January 31, the play opened at Ambassador Theatre in New York. Gladys Cooper acted as Mrs. Moore, Eric Portman as Fielding, Zia Mohyeddin as Aziz and Saed Jaffry as Professor Godbole. Santha Raryra Rau and her husband Faubion Bowers succeeded admirably. In presenting 'A Passage to India' in the dramatic form. Forster commented:

> I have always thought of my novels as novels and have never written them with any other medium in view. So it is a surprise as well as a pleasure to encounter this excellent and sensitive dramatic version of 'A Passage to India'.[34]

Forster is a living force in English fiction. According to Charles Richard Sanders, a work of art survives triumphantly because love, beauty and truth have the power of survival. Lytten Strachey's writings will be valued "for the steadfast love of art and beauty which they reflect; for the ideal of order which they embody in an age of confusion".[35] The views of Charles Richard Sanders, in respect of Lytten Strachey's writings, are perhaps also true of the novels of Forster which are characterized by a fresh outlook. The spontaneity of feeling, the warmth of human love, the sincerity and fluency of his philosophy, the awareness of the true self, the glow of the inner life, the loyalty to the inmost convictions and the allegiance to the spirit may be regarded as the positive values which are emphasized by Forster in his writings. In his novels, natural inclination is set against institutionalism; truth, against falsehood; appearance, against reality; sweet reasonableness against orthodoxy. In 'Anniversary Postscript,' Forster writes:

> "At the age of fifty he could recognize
> in Hitlerism an enemy of the heart as
> well as of the head and the arts."[36]

Forster believes in the "free movement of the mind which is necessary to the creative art",[37] he wants to "keep open a few breathing holes for the human spirit",[38] and he has faith in the aristocracy of talent - the "cultivated people are a drop of ink in the ocean".[39] In his subject-matter he has discovered the strength of thematic structure and the significance of the living symbol which conveys the meaning of life. He has succeeded in the form of fiction — social comedy, fantasy, and prophecy — to communicate his integrated vision of life. His novels strike a heartening note of optimism in "so stormy an age as ours" and they testify amply to his original outlook and his constant search for truth. A new technique coupled with an original outlook helps him to create an art form in fiction. His novels bear the stamp of his complex mind and leave behind a foaling of strange freshness like the Mosque of 'A Passage to India':

> There was nothing particular to look at — only old stones—but peace and happiness seemed to flow out and fill me.[40]

A passage to Forster is a difficult passage, but nevertheless a stimulating and exhilarating experience:

> .....; a passage, not easy, not now, not
> here, not to be apprehended except when

> it is unattainable: the God to be thrown
> was an emblem of that.[41]

There is always "a certain sense in an E.M. Forster novel of life's being rather more casual then it is, not flat, not mechanical, certainly not dull, but arbitrary some where day down; and in 'A Passage to India' sudden shafts of violence, of horror of death, and of the indifference of the living to the dead, are extremely effected".[42] While reading the novels of Forster we are made aware of the uncertainties of life. We have in his novels a sudden descent in to the dark depth of evil, and we have sudden raptures of joy. It is because of his moral philosophy, his imaginative vision of life, his penetrating insight, his intuitive knowledge of self and his own sensitiveness that his novels have acquired a deep meaning of life.

References

1. Crews, Frederick C.: E.M. Forster: The Perils of Humanism, (Princeton Univ. Press, 1962), p. 32.
2. Cox, C. B. : The Free Spirit (Oxford Univ. Press, 1963), p. 2.
3. *Ibid.*, p. 162.
4. Forster, E.M.: A Passage to India (London, Edward Arnold, 1924), p. 284.
5. Forster E.M. : Quoated by K. Natwar Singh in "A Passage of Broad Way." The Illustrated Weekly of India I, Vol. 32, 1962, p. 42.
6. Halloway, John: The Victorian Sage (London), p. 1.
7. Liddell, Rebert: Some Principles of Fiction (London), p. 1.
8. Crews, Fredorickc: The Perils of Humanism (Princeton Univ. Press 1962), p. 20.
9. Jones David : E.M. Forster on His Life and on His Books, An Interview Recorded for Television (The Listener, 1959) p. 12.
10. Tonybue Philip: Novel Through Forster's Classes (The Hindustan Times, 1959), p. 4.

11. Forster, E.M.: Aspect of the Novel (London, Edward Arnold, 1927), p. 48.
12. Toughes Philip: Novel Through Forster's Glasses (The Hindustan Time 1959), p. 1.
13. Haram, Aley : The Life and Thought of E.M. Forster (The Sunday Standard New Delhi, 1960), p. 31.
14. The Sunday Statesman: Writer's War (1962), p. 8.
15. Gold, Herbert: The Mystery of the Personality in the Novel (New York 1957), p. 101.
16. Forster's E.M. : A Passage to India (London, Edward Arnold 1924), p. 182.
17. Mair, Dewin : The Decline of the Novel; Essays on Literature and Society, 1949), p. 149.
18. Russell, Bertrand: Bertrand Russell, Conversation on BBC with John Freeman (The Listner Vol. 9, 1959), p. 504.
19. Allen, Glenn O: Structure, Symbol and Theme in Forster's A Passage to India, CPMLA, Vol.ixx, 1955), p. 954.
20. Forster, E.M. : Where Angels Fear to Tread (London Edward Arnold 1905), p. 150.
21. Forster's, E.M.: A Room with a View (London, Edward Arnold, 1908) p. 216.
22. Forster's, E.M.: Howard End (London, Edward Arnold, 1910), p. 307.
23. *Ibid.,* pp. 301,302.
24. Forster, E.M.: A Passage to India (London, Edward Arnold, 1924) p. 240.
25. Schweitzer, Albert: Indian Thought and Development (Wilne Ed. 1960), p. 107.
26. Cecil, David: Poet and Story Tellers (Constable, London, 1960), p. 193.
27. Forster, E.M.: A Passage to India (London Edward Arnold, 1924), p. 228.
28. *Ibid.,* pp. 174-75.
29. Forster, E.M. : Goldsworthy Lowes Dickinson (London 1934), p. 216.

30. Lerkin, Oliver, W. : Art and Life in America (New York, 1949), p. 461.
31. Zabel, Morten, D. : Craft and Character (London 1957), p. 237.
32. Woolf Virginia: Modern Fiction, The Common Reader (London 1948), p. 187.
33. Edel, Leon: The Psychologican Novel (London 1955), p. 142.
34. Forster, E.M. : Quoted by K. Natwar Singh in A Passage to India: The Illustrated.
35. Weekly of India, Vol. LXXX III, 1962, p. 42.
36. Sanders, Charles, R. : Lytton Strachey. His Mind and Art (Yale Univ. Press 1957), p. 353.
37. Forster, E.M. : Anniversary Postscript: A View Without A Room, The Hindustan Times Weekly, Sunday, Sep. 14, 1958.
38. Forster, E.M.: Two Cheers for Democracy, (London, Edward Arnold, 1951), p. 52.
39. Forster E.M. : Two Cheers for Democracy, What Would Germany to do us, p. 52.
40. Forster, E.M. : Two Cheers for Democracy, What I Believe, p. 81.
41. Forster, E.M. : Two Cheers for Democracy, The Last of Abinger, p. 367.
42. Forster, E.M.: A Passage to India, (London, Edward, Arnold, 1924), p. 309.

Bibliography

A. Secondary Sources: Selected Articles on E.M. Forster

Adult, P. : Aspect of Forster: Dublin Review, Vol. 219, 1946.

Allen, Glenn, O.: Structure, Symbol and theme in Forster's 'A Passage to India' : Modern Language Asso. of America, Vol. 70, 1955, p. 934.

Austin, Don: The Problem of Continuity of Three Novels of E.M. Forster, Modern Fiction Studies, Vol. 7, 1961.

Boyle, A.: Novels of Forster: Irish Monthly vol. 78 September 1950, pp. 405-415.

Brown, E.K.: The Revival of E.M. Forster: Yale Review, Vol. 33, 1944, pp. 668-681.

Clubb, R.L.: A Passage to India: The Meaning of Marubur Caves, College Association Journal, Vol. 6, 1963, p. 184-193.

Dauner, L.: What happened in the caves? Reflection on 'A Passage to India'. Modern Fiction Studies, Vol. 7, 1961, pp. 258-270.

Gilomen, W.: Fantasy and Prophesy in Forster's Work: E studies 27, 1946, pp. 97-112.

Hale, N. : A Passage to Relationship: Antilough Review, Vol. 20, 1960, pp. 172-180.

Lucas, J.: Wagner and Forster: Persifal an A Room with a

View, Journal of English Literary History" Vol. 53, March, 1966, p. 92-117.

Maclean, Huge: The Structure of *A Passage to India,* UTO, Vol. 22, 1953, pp. 157-171.

Marvey, John: Imagination and Moral Theme inE.M. Forster's The Longest Journey, E.C. Vol. 6, 1956.

McDowell, Fredrick, P.W.: The mild intellectual light the idea and theme in Howards End. Vol. 74, September, 1959, pp. 453-63.

Richard, I.A. : A Passage to Forster, Form 78-1927.

Shahane, V.A.: 'The Marabar Caves, Fact & Fiction, Amer Notes and Queries, Vol. 5, 1966.

Shanks, Edward: E.M. Forster: London, Mercury XVI, July 1927, pp. 265-74.

Thomson, G.H., 'Thematic Symbol in A Passage to India: 20th Century Literature, Vol. 7, No. 2, 1961.

Traversi, D.A.: The Novels of E.M. Forster, Arena, Vol. 1, 1937, pp. 28-40.

Westburg, Barry, R.: Forster's Fifth Symphony: Another Aspect of Howards End, Modern Fiction Studies, Vol. 10, 1964, pp. 359-65.

White, G.M.: "A Passage to India". Analysis and Revaluation, Vol. 68, September 1953, pp. 641-57.

Wilde, Alan: 'The Aesthetic View of Life', Where Angels Fear to Tread Modern Fiction Studies, Vol. 7, 1961, pp. 207-216.

B. Selected Critical Book on E.M. Forster

Allen, Walter: The English Novel, A short critical History, Penguin Books, 1965.

Beach, J.W. : The Twentieth Century, Novel Studies in Techniqe, Lyall Book Depot, Ludhiana Indian Edition, 1969.

Brander, Laurence: E.M. Forster — A Critical Study. Report Hart-Davis, London, 1968.

Beer, J.B. : The Achievement of E.M. Foster, Chatto & Windus, London, 1968.

Bradbury, Malcolm (ed). : A Passage to India: A Selection of critical Essays Casebook series, Macmillan, 1970.

Burback, A.S. (ed.): Techniques of Novel Writing. The Writer Inc. Boston, 1973.

Cecil, David: Poets and Story Tellers: A Book of Critical Essays, Constable London, 1960.

Crews, Frederich, C.: E.M. Forster: The Perils of Humanism: Princeton Univ. Press, 1962.

Colmer, John: E.M. Forster: The Personal Voice. Routledge & Kagan Paul, London & Boston, 1975.

Daiches, David: The Novels and the Modern World. Phoenix Books, 1965.

Fraser, G.S. : The Modern Writer and His World, Rupa & Co. Calcutta, 1961.

Godfrey, Danis: E.M. Forster's Other Kingdom. Oliver & Boyd, Edinburgh and London, 1962.

Gardiner, Philip (ed).: E.M. Forster: The Critical Heritage, Routledge and Kegan Paul: London & Boston, 1973.

James, Henry: The House of Fiction. Ed. & Intra by Leon Edcl Rupert Hart Davis, London, 1957.

Johnston, J.K. : The Blommsbury Group: A Study of E.M. Forster. Woolf and Their circle, New York. The Noonday Press, 1954.

Kettle, Arnold: An Introduction to the English Novel, Vols. I, II, Hutchinson's University Library, Huthinson House, London, W.J. New York, 1953.

Karl, Fredrick R. & Marvin Mangalaner : A Readers Guide to Great Twentieth Century English Novel. Thames & Hudson, London, 1973.

Leavis, F.R. : The Common Pursuit: A Peregrine Book, 1962.

Lever, Katherine: The Novel and the Reader. Methume & Co. Ltd. 36, Esse Street, London, WC. 1961.

Liddell, Robert: Some Principles of Fiction, Jonathan Cape Square London, 1956.

Langbaum Robert: The Modern Spirit, New York, Oxford Univ. Press, 1970.

Muir, Edwin: Structure of the Novel, Allied Publishers Pvt. Ltd. 1966.

McConkey, James: The Novels of E.M. Forster. Hthaka, Cornell University Press, 1957.

Macualay, Rose: The Writings of E.M. Forster, The Hogarth Press, London, Reprinted in 1970.

Oliver, H.J. : The Art of E.M. Forster, Melbourne, Melbourne Univ. Press, 1960.

Pritchett, V.S.: The Living Novel. Chatto & Windus, London, 1961.

Rose, Marfial: E.M. Forster. Erans Brothers Ltd. London, 1970.

Stallybrass, O. (Ed.): Aspect of E.M. Forster. Edward Arnold, 1966.

Stone, Wilfred: The Cave and The Mountain: A Study of E.M. Forster, Oxford Univ. Press, 1966.

Shahane, V.A. : E.M. Forster: A Study in Double Vision, Arnold Heinemann, New Delhi, 1975.

Syed, Hussain, Hamid (Ed.) : E.M. Forster: Only Connect, Letters to Indian Friends, New Delhi, Arnold Heinemann, 1979.

Singh, Avtar : The Novels of E.M. Forster, New Delhi, Atlantic Publishers and Distributors, 1986.

Trilling, Lionall: E.M. Forster, Norfold, Conn, New Directions Books, 1943.

Trilling, Lionall : The Liberal Imagination Essays on Literature and Society, Mercury, London, 1961.

Ward, A.C. : Twentieth Century Literature 1901-1940, Methuen & Co. Ltd. London, 36, Essex Street Strand WEZ, 1953.

Wool, F.V. : The Common Reader I Series, London, Hogarth Press, 1957.

Woolf, V.: The Common Reader II Series, London, Hogarth Press, 1964.

Wilde, Alan: Art and Order: A Study of E.M. Forster, Peter Oven, London, 1965.

Zabel, Mocton, Danwen Craft and Character in Modern Fiction, New York: Viking Press, 1957.

Index